Race, Class, and Social welfare

What makes it so difficult to enact and sustain comprehensive social welfare policy that would aid the disadvantaged in the United States? Addressing the relationship between populism and social welfare, this book argues that two competing camps of populists divide American politics. Regressive populists motivated by racial resentment frequently clash with progressive populists, who embrace an expansion of social welfare benefits for the less affluent, regardless of race or ethnicity. Engstrom and Huckfeldt uncover the political forces driving this divided populism, its roots in the aftermath of the civil rights revolution of the mid-twentieth century, and its implications for modern American politics and social welfare policy. Relying on a detailed analysis of party coalitions in the US Congress and the electorate since the New Deal, the authors focus on the intersection between race, class, and oligarchy.

Erik J. Engstrom is Professor of Political Science, University of California, Davis. He is the author of *Partisan Gerrymandering and the Construction of American Democracy* (2013) and co-author of *Party Ballots, Reform, and the Transformation of America's Electoral System* (2014). The latter was the co-winner of the 2015 J. David Greenstone Prize for best book in Politics and History from the American Political Science Association.

Robert Huckfeldt is Distinguished Professor Emeritus, Department of Political Science, University of California, Davis. He is the author or co-author of a series of journal articles and books, including most recently *Experts, Activists, and Interdependent Citizens* with T. K. Ahn and John Barry Ryan. He was elected to the American Academy of Arts and Sciences in 2014.

Race, Class, and Social Welfare

American Populism Since the New Deal

ERIK J. ENGSTROM

University of California, Davis

ROBERT HUCKFELDT

University of California, Davis

CAMBRIDGE
UNIVERSITY PRESS

CAMBRIDGE
UNIVERSITY PRESS

Shaftesbury Road, Cambridge CB2 8EA, United Kingdom

One Liberty Plaza, 20th Floor, New York, NY 10006, USA

477 Williamstown Road, Port Melbourne, VIC 3207, Australia

314–321, 3rd Floor, Plot 3, Splendor Forum, Jasola District Centre, New Delhi – 110025, India

103 Penang Road, #05–06/07, Visioncrest Commercial, Singapore 238467

Cambridge University Press is part of Cambridge University Press & Assessment, a department of the University of Cambridge.

We share the University's mission to contribute to society through the pursuit of education, learning and research at the highest international levels of excellence.

www.cambridge.org
Information on this title: www.cambridge.org/9781108819459

DOI: 10.1017/9781108873116

First published 2020
First paperback edition 2022

A catalogue record for this publication is available from the British Library

ISBN   978-1-108-83692-0   Hardback
ISBN   978-1-108-81945-9   Paperback

To Mary Engstrom and Sharon Huckfeldt

Contents

Figures

Tables

Preface and Acknowledgments

Many Americans experienced a rude shock on the evening of November 8, 2016, when they learned that Donald Trump would become the next president of the United States. Similarly, it had been surprising for many Americans, Republicans and Democrats alike, when Donald Trump fashioned a successful populist campaign that accumulated a string of victories in Republican primaries and ultimately secured the party's nomination at the 2016 Republican National Convention. This book argues that we should not have been caught off guard. Indeed, populist appeals are deeply embedded in the history of the Republic, and a wide variety of successful populist appeals have played influential roles in the history of its politics.

Some of these populist programs and appeals, such as Franklin Roosevelt's New Deal, have been progressive efforts aimed at improving the political and economic fortunes of everyday Americans. Other reactionary populist appeals, most famously in the American South but elsewhere as well, have successfully employed political messages anchored in animosity based on race and class.

Most recently, we can see the consequences of reactionary, upside-down populist appeals with respect to social welfare policy in American politics. That is, those who need social welfare legislation the most – the economically disadvantaged – are often least likely to support it. This has clearly been the case in the vitriolic debate over the Affordable Care Act (ACA), but the problem certainly predates the difficult history of the ACA. Indeed, opposition to the expansion of the social welfare state is frequently pronounced among lower-income white voters – many of whom would be ultimate beneficiaries. We argue that the solution to this puzzle lies deeply ingrained within the conjoint dynamics of race and class in American life and hence in American politics.

We are particularly grateful to a number of colleagues who have supported us in this effort. Two former graduate students, Jack Reilly and Fan Lu, have been supportive throughout, and each has been a collaborator on one of the chapters (Chapters 4 and 5, respectively). We have also benefitted from the insights and advice gained from a series of colleagues: Ted Carmines, Carol Kohfeld, Ben Highton, Walt Stone, Chris Hare, Franz Pappi, Ron Rapoport, Matt Pietryka, and John Ryan. Carol Kohfeld, Paul Sniderman, John Sprague, and two anonymous reviewers read the complete manuscript and made particularly helpful suggestions.

American Politics and Social Welfare

Donald Trump appeared to turn American politics upside down in his 2016 presidential election campaign. He accomplished this feat by embracing issues that have long been at the core of Republican Party platforms and combining them with positions that appealed to socially, economically, and politically disaffected white voters. In addition to advocating a pro-life agenda, he reached out to traditional Republican constituencies in a range of important ways, embracing tax reform and tax cuts as well as promising major rollbacks of Obama-era regulatory regimes that were aimed at reversing climate change, stimulating economic competition, and stabilizing financial markets. Perhaps most importantly, he promised to repeal and replace the Affordable Care Act (ACA) – the most important social welfare legislation adopted since the establishment of Medicare in 1965. All these positions fall in line with Republican orthodoxy regarding small government and unfettered free enterprise.

At the same time, other of Trump's positions and promises were aimed at appealing to disaffected whites in ways that seemingly contradicted traditional Republican doctrine. Free trade regimes and ready access to the supply of foreign workers have long been important issues to core supporters of the Republican Party, but he broke with those traditions by advocating punitive restrictions on immigration and trade. In particular, he promised to abandon Obama's commitment to the relaxed trade restrictions of the proposed Trans-Pacific Partnership, to reconsider trade agreements established with Canada and Mexico in the North American Free Trade Agreement of 1994, and to construct aggressive restrictions on both legal and illegal immigration, not only from Mexico but from other countries as well. In short, by embracing new and robust restrictions on trade and immigration, Trump turned his back on the internationalist wing of the Republican Party with a populist appeal aimed at politically disgruntled voters among working-class and lower-middle-class whites.

Many professional politicians, both Democrats and Republicans, were caught flat-footed and flummoxed in their efforts to respond. Similarly, many scholars and pundits were also puzzled by Trump's nomination and eventual victory. This book argues that they should not have been surprised. Trump is certainly not the first politically conservative politician to employ racial animus and scare tactics as wedge issues aimed at fracturing a working-class coalition.

This book is not primarily focused on the election of Donald Trump, even though Chapter 8 is devoted to an analysis of the political coalitions and issues that led to his election. Rather, we are primarily concerned with the political and historical contexts and processes that made the election of Donald Trump possible. Trump successively employed a regressive form of populism – a populist appeal aimed at dividing rather than unifying working-class voters. Regressive populism is nothing new to American politics. At least since the end of the American Civil War, political demagogues have employed race and ethnicity as wedge issues aimed at undermining working-class coalitions (Key 1949; Woodward 1938). In doing so, they have frequently succeeded in turning populism upside down, creating working-class coalitions that oppose rather than support the extension of social welfare benefits.

More than a century earlier, the German sociologist Werner Sombart addressed the general issue in his 1905 effort, *Why Is There No Socialism in the United States?* Sombart's question has guided generations of scholars in analyzing the past, present, and future of American politics. At the time that Sombart wrote, European social democracies were being formed that have now persisted through two world wars, governments of the left and the right, and severe economic crises. Perhaps contrary to the expectations of Sombart and others, social democracy – defined as the government's direct or indirect provision of social welfare services – has grown and prospered in western European democracies without government appropriation of the means of production. Thus, it is possible to pursue social welfare absent socialism (Stiglitz 2012: 163).

At the same time, the United States' progress in the public provision of social services has been slow, halting, and frequently reversed. Among OECD (Organisation for Economic Co-operation and Development) countries, the United States currently ranks twenty-one out of thirty-six in social welfare spending as a percentage of GDP (gross domestic product) (OECD 2019). Indeed, President Trump's first action in office was to issue an executive order weakening enforcement of the ACA. Thus, a modern version of Sombart's question, and the focal question of our book, is this: What factors make it so difficult to enact and sustain comprehensive social welfare policy in the United States?

Sombart and the scholars who pursue this question have offered a laundry list of explanations for the American social welfare failures. But the one that continues to have the most explanatory power, we argue, is the racial animosity that has often fractured the political potential of the American working class. Thus, we see a disjuncture between what we term progressive and regressive populism. Progressive populists embrace an expansion of social welfare benefits for the less affluent regardless of race or ethnicity. Regressive populists, by contrast, are unwilling to support social welfare benefits that extend to racial and ethnic minorities.

From this perspective, Trump is only one among a long and substantial historical list of regressive populist politicians who have successfully manipulated this racial divide to fracture working-class politics in America. He shares his place on the list with both subtle and notorious race-baiters from American political history such as Mississippi's Theodore Bilbo and Alabama's George Wallace. Indeed, the race card is played widely, even by seemingly respectable American politicians who continue to be held in high repute (Gilens 1996; Mendelberg 2001).

ARE CULTURE WARS RESPONSIBLE?

An alternative way to view these problems regarding populism and social welfare is in terms of a cultural divide that has evolved into a series of culture wars. One part of the population has embraced same-sex marriage, abortion rights, secularization, and racial-ethnic diversity. Another part of the population has embraced what have come to be called traditional moral values. And the end product has been rancorous divisions based on deeply held beliefs that are extremely difficult to bridge. The Democratic Party has generally (but not uniformly) adopted more sympathetic positions regarding the rights of gays, the freedom of choice to terminate pregnancies, and a range of other morally contested issues. Hence, the argument becomes that a moral rebellion against the party most closely aligned with these newer values has become a deeply polarizing culture war (Edsall 2015; Inglehart and Norris 2017; Williamson 2016).

Such an argument corresponds well with the established literature on postmaterial values in advanced democratic societies (Dalton 2018, 2019; Inglehart 1977; Inglehart and Norris 2017). That is, rising affluence has turned the attention of many citizens away from issues related to economics and material insecurity, focusing instead on nonmaterial issues related to personal freedom and moral issues. And thus, as a consequence, the class basis of politics has been displaced by a new set of issues that revolve around fundamental moral and lifestyle issues.

Several problems arise with respect to this diagnosis. First, material insecurity is broadly distributed within the American population, and it is not limited to a single ethnic, religious, racial, or cultural grouping. Poverty is persistent among whites as well as among people of color, and thus, even relatively affluent whites might harbor credible concerns regarding the well-being of their children. Hence, citizens of every racial and ethnic group confront issues related to their material well-being and the provision of adequate social services, but disadvantaged whites are much less likely than disadvantaged African Americans to vote for candidates who advocate expanded social welfare services. Absent racial hostility, it becomes difficult to explain why less affluent whites would act on the basis of postmaterial values, while less affluent nonwhites would act on the basis of material concerns.

Moreover, the political boundaries separating Democrats, Republicans, liberals, and conservatives do not map neatly onto these economic or cultural divides. Affluence and poverty cross the boundaries between regular church attenders and religious skeptics, and they are found within both parties and both sets of ideologies. Moreover, traditional morality is not wholly confined within the boundaries of either party or ideology. While we are not ignoring the role of these cultural divides in polarizing the population, it is important to remember that Hillary Clinton won sizeable majorities of black fundamentalists, and Donald Trump won sizeable majorities among white fundamentalists. In short, we are certainly not arguing that beliefs and cultural values are politically inconsequential, and neither do we believe that they lie at the heart of the matter. They are, rather, important but secondary phenomena in their relationship to the political process.

In explaining the failure of social welfare policy in American politics, our attention turns toward the particular features of American political institutions, the changing structure of party coalitions, and the underlying political and economic relations among groups in American politics.

ECONOMIC CLASS IN AMERICAN POLITICS

The disgruntled whites who are vulnerable to manipulative racial appeals frequently have compelling reasons for their political disaffection. It has been a difficult fifty years for working-class and lower-middle-class Americans *of all racial and ethnic groups*. Advances in automation and related production technologies have meant that many well-paying jobs in factories and on assembly lines have disappeared. At the same time, a great deal of low-skill employment has migrated offshore to inexpensive labor markets. Hence, working-class and middle-class Americans are being squeezed by technology, on the one hand, and low wage scales in third-world countries, on the other.

Not coincidentally, all this has been happening at the same time that unions, unionization, and union membership are in steep decline. Labor unions are severely diminished as influential voices, not only with respect to wages and working conditions but also with respect to relevant domestic issues in American politics. Two primary exceptions are the SEIU (Service Employees International Union) and AFSCME (American Federation of State, County and Municipal Employees) – two unions that primarily represent state and local government employees. The problem is that their successes have sometimes discredited their reputations as being unions that fund political campaigns, receiving pay raises and employee benefits in return, thus creating resentment that serves to compromise the union movement further.

As a consequence, income inequality has increased dramatically during this period, not only in the United States (Bartels 2008; Piketty and Saez 2003; Stiglitz 2012) but internationally as well (Piketty 2014). Indeed, the difficult circumstances facing working-class and lower-middle-class workers have become increasingly grim, and the problem is not entirely unique to any single racial group or any single country. Moreover, refugee migrations into western Europe have begun to create similar fractures and fissures within the working-class base of support for the traditional social welfare state. The problem has been especially severe in the United States, however, for reasons related to particular features of American politics and political institutions.

Hence, Trump's strategy was to broaden the base of the Republican Party's traditionally conservative coalition by embracing social groups whose political loyalties, fifty years earlier, had been closely linked to the Democratic Party. This is not, in itself, an entirely new idea. At least since Disraeli introduced nineteenth-century social welfare legislation, the tradition of "working-class Tories" has been a historically familiar phenomenon. Conservative prime minister Disraeli managed to peel off support from the Liberal Party in much the same way that Bismarck managed to peel off support from the Social Democrats in the newly unified German state. None of this transgresses the principles or practice of democratic politics, but the process becomes toxic when racial divisions come into play.

Closer to home in both space and time, Ronald Reagan famously cultivated support among normally Democratic working-class voters – the so-called Reagan Democrats. And at repeated moments, he played the race card in appealing to white working-class voters, making only slightly veiled references to "welfare queens."

Trump's appeal during the 2016 campaign was similarly embedded within a clear racial message. "Making America Great Again" is not an appealing message to groups who are attempting to overcome patterns of racial and ethnic bias deeply embedded in American history. Indeed, for many voters, it was a look backward, pointing to a past marked by Jim Crow; racial injustice; and patterns of discrimination anchored in race, ethnicity, and national origin. Hence, the major themes of the Trump campaign, as well as his actions as the president, have failed to respond to the needs and aspirations of citizens of color. Rather, he has focused on securing his base among disaffected whites in conjunction with support for a traditional Republican program of tax cuts and deregulation.

POPULISM'S OBSTACLES

As a consequence of Trump's appeal to disaffected, economically disadvantaged voters, he has been widely characterized as a populist. And populism has been widely associated with white, racially motivated voters. In his comprehensive analysis of Trump's Republican Party, Luce (2017) frames the issue as one in which populism is undermining the basis of liberal democracy. An important part of our argument is that liberal democracy and populist democracy are not necessarily in conflict. Instead, they are integral component parts of a healthy democratic politics. And indeed, an important aspect of liberal democratic politics is that all legitimate interests and groups, including disadvantaged members of the working class and lower middle class, have a place and a voice in the political marketplace of claims and expectations.

A primary problem is that some groups have been left out and left behind, and these groups are the ones most likely to benefit from populist social welfare policies. The excluded groups include coal miners, unemployed and underemployed workers in the industrial belt, service workers in fast-food chains, and more. And these groups span racial and ethnic divides: white, black, Latino American, and Asian. Regardless of their shared interests, however, these groups have failed to coalesce politically.

The question thus arises, why has this failure occurred? Conservative populist appeals have frequently and skillfully exploited racial antagonism both to defeat efforts at constructing multiracial coalitions and to defeat efforts at extending social welfare benefits. Trump's Republican Party does not include citizens of color as a meaningful part of its base, and he stokes the fires of racial antagonism. He equates neo-Nazis with civil rights demonstrators. He attacks NFL (National Football League) players and owners when players supporting Black Lives Matter respectfully take a knee during the playing of the national anthem. In short, he exploits racial-ethnic hostility as a primary weapon in his political arsenal.

Efforts aimed at fragmenting the populist base are not new to American politics. Such efforts began before the ink was dry on the Emancipation Proclamation, and they continued throughout the era of reconstruction (Foner 1988; Foner and Brown 2005) and into twentieth-century politics (Woodward 1938). American political history is replete with instances of strategic politicians fomenting racial competition in an effort to racially divide the populist base (Key 1949). In this context, Donald Trump adds to a long tradition of politically invoked racial tensions that have impeded the progress of social welfare legislation in American politics.

For our purposes, populism is defined in the context of the early work by Woodward and others who focused on the potential for an appeal based on class interests independent of race and ethnicity. Such an agenda served as the original motivation for Tom Watson's foray into southern populist politics, but when this effort failed, he joined the southern tradition of race-baiters who pursued the strategy of politically manipulating and dividing blacks from disadvantaged whites (Woodward 1938).

The historical problem in American politics is that a populist political effort has never managed to construct an enduring class-based populist appeal that has unified blacks and whites. The zenith of the populist movement was, of course, in the 1896 nomination of the Populist William Jennings Bryan as the presidential candidate of the Democratic Party. Creating a biracial coalition played no part in Bryan's efforts, however, and populism ultimately failed in the South because of the threat it posed to white racial hegemony. Bryan had the support of the southern Democrats, and he benefitted from the disfranchisement of African Americans (Woodward 1938: 150–153). Indeed, the solid white Democratic South depended on the expulsion of African Americans from participation in Democratic Party politics.

Liberal democratic politics presupposes that all legitimate interests are represented within the political process, and populism expresses the interests of citizens who are disadvantaged relative to the remainder of the population. Populism simply acknowledges that "we the people" – the words that begin the Constitution's preamble – represents the commitment that all the people should be represented within the democratic process. The problem is that contemporary American politics suffers from a deficiency of organized interests representing such a legitimate populist viewpoint. To paraphrase Hubert Humphrey, the moral test of government is measured in terms of the manner in which it treats old people, young people, and poor people. And the question thus arises, why is our liberal democracy failing to represent those interests?

Part of the answer revolves around racial antagonisms. Many Americans who desperately need medical care, and indeed are eligible to receive it through the ACA, nevertheless applaud President Trump's efforts to end the program. Why? Many see the ACA as a program supporting a population that is unworthy of support, where worth is defined by racial and ethnic stereotypes.

Another part of the difficulty revolves around well-known collective action problems (Olson 1965). In particular, it is often easier to mobilize small groups rather than large ones. Smaller groups are more likely to depend on the support of each member's appreciable contribution to the group effort. In contrast, the success of groups involving larger numbers of members does not depend on the contribution of any single individual. No single contribution is vital to the success of the group, and hence, members are less likely to recognize the urgency of their own contribution. A cascade of nonsupport and free riding is thus produced.

Thus, it is relatively easy to secure the material support of major oil companies for the American Petroleum Institute's lobbying efforts on behalf of big oil. In contrast, it is much more difficult to secure the support of social welfare recipients for lobbying activities on behalf of the ACA. The participation of ExxonMobil is crucial to the first effort. The participation of any single social welfare recipient is not crucial to the second.

Hence, we confront a well-known paradox of democratic politics. Liberal democracies thrive when all interests are represented. The problem is that democratic political systems have a built-in bias that, paradoxically, rewards the interests of small groups sharing particular interests and penalizes large groups with widely shared common interests.

PARTY FAILURES

Just as important, the widely shared populist interests of large groups are sometimes poorly served by the institutionally defined dynamics of the single-member congressional districts that give rise to American two-party politics. The persistent dilemma confronting both professional politicians and centrist party supporters in any two party political system is the danger of capture by a party's more ideologically committed constituencies. Indeed, the continuing drama within any two-party system is the struggle between moderate and ideologically committed supporters. The strategic goal of the moderates is to define the party and its candidates with a broad appeal capable of succeeding in winner-take-all electoral contests. In contrast, the goal of the more ideologically committed voters is to make their voices heard both within intraparty politics in the formation of party platforms and positions and in the nomination of party candidates.

In his analysis of two-party political systems, Anthony Downs established an analytically compelling account of the spatial logic underlying the ideologically moderate politics of the 1950s. As he demonstrated, parties and their candidates are motivated to pursue the median voters who will provide the winning votes in elections. And since they are able to ignore their more extreme supporters who have no political alternative, both parties pursue many of the same moderate voters occupying the middle of the political spectrum. These are, indeed, the only voters likely to be persuaded, and hence the model predicts that the parties will converge on moderate, practical policies that will win majority support within the electorate.

The problems of two-party politics become more severe in the context of political competition that is motivated by both race and class. As Benoit and Shepsle (1995) demonstrate, racial bloc voting – and particularly the refusal of whites to vote for black candidates – effectively dilutes minority representation. Moreover, racial bloc voting guarantees victory for candidates of the districts' racial majorities, *regardless of candidate locations on ideological or policy dimensions*. The problem can be exacerbated by the creation of majority-minority districts aimed at securing the election of representatives who belong to racial minorities (Cameron, Epstein, and O'Halloran 1996; Guinier 1992). While the creation of these districts furthers the goal of increasing the number of elected minority group representatives, its cost often comes in the currency of underrepresenting substantive, class-based interests such as those related to social welfare.

Not only do elections register preferences of voters in two-party systems but these elections also serve to aggregate the preferences of voters into a majority coalition. In contrast, voters in multiparty systems are *not* responsible for forming majority coalitions. Rather, they simply register their support for one of several parties, and the relevant party leaders are the ones who, in turn, aggregate voters' preferences by joining a political coalition that is likely to involve multiple parties.

The spatial model is often helpful in explaining the outcome of elections once the candidates are chosen. Indeed, it performed reasonably well throughout the 1950s in explaining American electoral politics. The model provides less guidance regarding the problematic consequences for candidate selection. That is, there is no guarantee that parties will select candidates who are well positioned to address the concerns of the median voter in the electorate as a whole.

The implicit assumption is that a party's supporters aim to select the candidate with the best chance of winning the general election. A problem frequently arises because many voters are *not* typically motivated by any objectively informed calculation regarding probable outcomes in the general election. Rather, they are primarily motivated by their own political interests and preferences, and these may or may not translate into the selection of a politically competitive candidate. Hence, they often pursue their own compelling concerns with something that appears, at least among their opponents, to be reckless abandon. Intraparty struggles frequently occur between two groups: (1) the highly motivated supporters of more ideologically extreme candidates and (2) the party professionals and more moderate rank-and-file party supporters whose primary goal is to win the general election.

In 2016, both parties experienced different versions of this dynamic tension among different groups of supporters. Within the Democratic Party, the tension was between the moderately liberal Democrats who supported Hillary Clinton and the more extremely liberal Democrats who supported free college tuition, income equality, stricter government regulation of Wall Street, and the candidacy of Bernie Sanders. Among Republicans, the primary tension was between the moderately conservative Republicans who supported one of several moderately conservative candidates and the more extremely right-wing, regressive populists who ultimately coalesced in support of Donald Trump, building a wall along the Mexican border and creating trade barriers that keep jobs in America. In short, Donald Trump did not resemble the traditional pro-file of a conservative Republican, and many conservative Republicans were unwilling to identify him as a member of the same political party.

Hence, both parties confronted their own versions of populist rebellions in 2016 – populist rebellions that lay at opposite ends of the underlying ideological dimension. Bernie Sanders and Donald Trump each offered an appeal to what they characterized as the overlooked interests of everyday voters within the electorate. Hillary Clinton, the establishment candidate within the Democratic Party, was able to surmount the Sanders' challenge, but she was only marginally successful at connecting with many of the Sanders' supporters who would have normally been expected to provide unswerving loyalty to the Democratic Party candidate – younger African Americans and blue-collar workers in the rust belt states. In contrast, Donald Trump was not the first choice of many traditionally conservative Republican voters, but he managed to win respectable levels of support within the party's rank and file, combined with substantial levels of sup-port among white working-class voters who might have been expected to support the Democratic candidate, at least in times past.

In both instances, the professional politicians coalesced around their more moderate party candidates. Democratic office holders were likely to support Clinton, and Republican office holders were more likely to support almost anyone but Trump. There were exceptions, particularly among the Republicans, but in the first years of the Trump presidency, there continued to be a substantial subset of Republican office holders who sought to save the party from the Trump brand.

Perhaps the most notable example of this effort occurred when two former Republican presidents, George H. W. Bush and George W. Bush, released the joint statement that "Americans must always reject racial bigotry, anti-Semitism, and hatred in all forms" (Prignano 2017). Their statement came the day after President Trump's statement suggesting that neo-Nazi protestors in Charlottesville were comparable to others who were protesting against the denial of civil rights. In short, the two Bush presidents were engaged in a salvage mission aimed at protecting their Republican Party brand.

The irony, at least within the Downs' framework, is that the candi-date who would have appeared to be farthest away from the median voter, Donald Trump, won not only his party's nomination but the general election as well. Part of this, we argue, is because both par-ties have been unable to respond satisfactorily to their own versions of a populist rebellion among rank-and-file supporters. The prominent populist vision among liberal Democrats tilts toward social welfare and strong support for the rights of women and minorities. The populist vision among Republicans tilts toward religious fundamentalism and a nativism that rebels against what is viewed as the privileged treatment of racial and ethnic minorities. The Democratic Party managed to colonize Wall Street, but many rank-and-file Democrats were deeply suspicious of a party that embraced free trade and relied on campaign funds from a wealthy donor class. Many rank-and-file Republicans were equally suspicious of their own party for a lack of progress on the grassroots issues with which they were concerned – job creation, immigration barriers, and a set of issues that revolve around personal morality.

In short, both parties have struggled in responding to their own populist insurgencies, and these challenges to party control are motivated by overlapping sets of concerns. In particular, both Democrats and Republicans of modest means have deeply experienced economic decline as national income has become increasingly concentrated in the upper reaches of the income scale (Bartels 2008; Piketty and Saez 2003). Working-class wages have stagnated, and many low-skilled but well-compensated jobs have disappeared. The cost of college tuition continues to increase more rapidly than inflation. Medical care and medical insurance continue to be prohibitively expensive for many individuals. And many traditional working-class communities are in decline.

While these populist revolts within the major parties respond to many of the same underlying factors, they have produced radically different political responses and policy proposals. Hence, the challenges are authentic with especially severe consequences among lower-income groups. The underlying problem is that the economically threatened groups are badly divided – not only politically but also racially, ethnically, socially, and geographically – with politically debilitating consequences. Hence, our argument is threefold.

First, these divisions among economically threatened groups prevent the translation of shared interests into political progress in addressing underlying problems related to social welfare. And indeed, these divisions are magnified in the American political system with single-member districts and winner-take-all elections. Second, these divisions are not new but to the contrary are rooted in the political and social history of the nation. And finally, the future of American politics depends on an adequate response to the problems that confront the social welfare of these threatened groups – both Democratic and Republican. The social, economic, and political prosperity of the nation depends on the quality of the national investment in human and social capital. And such an investment is currently being hindered by a political failure to respond to these underlying political challenges.

What stands in the way of a unified populist agenda? We argue that the problem lies at the intersection of race, class, and oligarchy. One hundred and fifty years of progress in addressing the free exercise of citizenship rights by all American citizens has been pivotal to American democracy. The problem that remains is an electorate that remains deeply divided by *both* race *and* class and hence is vulnerable to its own worst antidemocratic instincts, as well as to elite domination.

Once again, these are not new problems. A great many Americans were shocked to see Donald Trump elected to the presidency, but the roots of the underlying dynamic that propelled him to victory can be seen quite vividly in America's political history. In the chapters that follow, we consider the incomplete reconstruction of American politics following the end of slavery, the ongoing patterns of hostility toward non-European immigrants, the resulting fracture of a class-based populism in American politics, the consequences of social and economic change for the party coalitions, and the long-term electoral implications of the civil rights revolution for the parties, for Congress, and for the electorate.

This book examines the transformation of political arrangements in American politics that has undermined the development of social welfare policy. Rather than being organized by economic interests, the American electorate is increasingly fragmented by race, ethnicity, and national origin. The implications for politics and policy are profound and far-reaching, particularly in the context of the increased concentration of wealth and political influence within economic and political elites. The implications become particularly vivid within the American working class, with deep divisions based on race and ethnic origin. These deep divisions lie not only at the heart of a divided working class but also in the larger structure of party politics and the institutional representation of interests within the political process.

AN OUTLINE OF THE ARGUMENT

In the chapters that follow, we address these questions in two politically dynamic settings: (1) the dramatically altered institutional context of American politics, particularly with respect to the US Congress, and (2) the transformed electoral context arising because of social and demographic change within the electorate combined with internal and external patterns of migration.

Chapter 2 addresses the complex interdependence that has evolved among race, class, and oligarchy in American politics, as well as locating the broad historical sweep of events that has brought us to the present moment in American politics. Neither of the authors are professional historians, but as political scientists, we believe that current dilemmas of American politics are rooted in historical context. And subsequent chapters address these historical processes and events with the analytic tools of political science.

Chapter 3 considers the underlying political tensions and contradictions that have persisted within American populism, as well as the profound implications for civil rights and social welfare policy. American political institutions have not been equal to the task of simultaneously furthering the causes of both civil rights and social welfare policy.

Chapter 4 gives detailed attention to the rise of civil rights on the congressional agenda, with particular attention focused on the adoption of the 1957 Civil Rights Act – the most important civil rights legislation passed in more than a half-century and a critical turning point in the evolution of American parties and political coalitions.

Chapters 5 and 6 address the eclipse of the New Deal coalition and the resulting implications for American political parties in both the Senate and the House of Representatives. The Republican Party's southern strategy converted the South from being the most Democratic region of the country into the most Republican. And the basis of support for social welfare policy was dramatically undermined within this process.

Chapter 7 analyzes the end result of institutional changes that have effectively turned populism and the support for social welfare benefits upside down. In the post–World War II period of American politics, support for social welfare policy came from a populist impulse generated primarily by working-class whites and labor unions. Twenty years later, union members and working-class whites had dramatically declined as a significant proportion of both the population and the Democratic coalition. The party of the working class and social welfare was rapidly becoming dependent on votes from both the white middle class and racial and ethnic minorities.

Chapter 8 considers the shape and composition of the electoral coalitions in contemporary American politics with respect to the 2016 presidential election. In particular, we focus on the implications of conservative white populism and hostility to the ACA that underlie the electoral success of Donald Trump.

Finally, Chapter 9 concludes by considering the basis of the party coalitions, the implications for contemporary politics, and the future of social welfare policy and American politics.

2

Politics at the Intersection of Race, Class, and Oligarchy

The events leading to the adoption of key civil rights and voting rights legislation in the 1950s, 1960s, and 1970s came at a critical moment in American political history – a moment that preserved the legitimacy of the American political system. Absent those events, denials of citizenship rights based on race and ethnicity would have been sustained in large parts of the country, the "Second Revolution" in American politics (McPherson 1992) would have been aborted, and the United States would have ceased to qualify as a democracy. The efforts and sacrifices made at Antietam in 1862, Gettysburg in 1863, Ford's Theater in 1865, Little Rock in 1957, Birmingham in 1963, Selma in 1965, and at other countless places and times would have been wasted. Moreover, the transforming potential of the due process, equal protection, and citizenship guarantees of the Thirteenth, Fourteenth, and Fifteenth Amendments would have gone unrealized. In short, absent the significant political and legislative accomplishments that occurred as a consequence of those struggles, it would have been impossible to begin the long process of unraveling homegrown institutions of American apartheid.

Support for systems of apartheid was common not only in the American South but also among others in American politics opposed to racial egalitarianism. In a 1957 *National Review* article, "Why the South Must Prevail," William F. Buckley argued that the white race was more advanced and fit to govern, defending both the right of whites to govern even when they constituted a minority of the population, as well as their right to discriminate against African Americans (Felzenberg 2017, 79–80). The racial and political parallels between white South Africa and the American South were not lost on contemporary observers of American politics, even if the severity of the problem and potential for progress differed. Buckley's views evolved over time, as he moved toward a more sympathetic view of the civil rights movement, partially in response to his own distaste toward the rise of regressive populists such as the then Alabama governor George Wallace. Times have changed, and support for racial segregation (apartheid) as a matter of principle has declined, but segregation in American life has deep roots documented by Massey and Denton (1998) in *American Apartheid.*

The problem is that victories over racial and ethnic segregation and discrimination, as well as progress in reducing obstacles to economic opportunity among the disadvantaged, remain incomplete. Stark social and economic disparities continue to exist, and economic inequality continues to increase (Bartels 2008; Hacker and Pierson 2010; Piketty and Saez 2003). Moreover, these economic problems are not isolated within particular racial and ethnic groups. Dramatic economic transformations have left increasing numbers of Americans of all races and ethnicities in difficult economic circumstances, frequently at the margins of American society, without even minimally adequate social, medical, and educational services.

THE PERSISTING PROBLEM: DIVERGENT DEFINITIONS OF POPULISM

Most recently, candidates of both the major parties in the 2016 presidential election constructed an appeal aimed at economically disadvantaged voters. Hillary Clinton framed a message directed toward the social, cultural, and environmental concerns of many liberals, as well as a focus on economic concerns that were particularly attractive to African Americans, Latino Americans, and other racial and ethnic minorities. Her campaign had more difficulty directing an appeal toward the white working class. At one town hall meeting during the campaign, she seemed to promise that she would run coal miners out of business. Her statement invited being taken out of its accompanying context, and it generated a damaging self-inflicted wound.

Look, we have serious economic problems in many parts of our country.... Instead of dividing people the way Donald Trump does, let's reunite around policies that will bring jobs and opportunities to all these underserved poor communities. So for example, I'm the only candidate which has a policy about how to bring economic opportunity using clean renewable energy as the key into coal country. Because we're going to put a lot of coal miners and coal companies out of business . . . . And we're going to make it clear that we don't want to forget those people. Those people labored in those mines for generations, losing their health, often losing their lives to turn on our lights and power our factories. (Transcript of Hillary Clinton at a CNN Town Hall in Columbus, Ohio, March 13, 2016)

The statement was clearly a political misstep, and Clinton quickly regretted making it. The statement is particularly important, not only because it was a notable "gotcha" moment in the campaign. Indeed, the campaign was full of these moments, such as the "Access Hollywood" tape in which Trump recounted his exploits in grabbing female genitalia. Why did Clinton's misstep take on political significance while Trump's was dismissed?

Clinton's appeal to the economically disadvantaged tended to treat disadvantaged whites as a subset of the larger group, which of course they are. The problem is that the Democratic Party is seen among many of these whites as giving unwarranted attention to African Americans, Latino Americans, and other minority groups. Many others probably object to being classified as members of the "underserved poor communities." Indeed, many members of nonwhite groups are likely to feel ill at ease being classified as members of the underserved poor. In short, the Democratic Party rose to prominence on the definition of a politically empowered and unified working-class base, but that base is vulnerable to its own increasing levels of racial and ethnic heterogeneity, and it is particularly vulnerable to white working-class resentment.

In contrast, Donald Trump's campaign was organized along two primary fronts: an appeal aimed at traditionally conservative Republican voters who embraced tax cuts and reduced regulations for business as well as a strident populist appeal aimed primarily at the political empowerment of disaffected working-class whites. In pursuing this second populist appeal, he broke with traditional Republican orthodoxy, rejecting liberalized international trade regimes and condemning businesses that outsourced manufacturing jobs to other countries. His promise was simple, direct, and extremely appealing to many members of the white working class. "Making America Great Again" came to mean (1) the return of well-paid jobs allegedly being lost to Mexico, Canada, China, and Southeast Asia; (2) building a wall to stop the flow of illegal immigrants, who were accused of committing crimes and taking jobs away from Americans; and (3) cutting regulations alleged to be slowing economic growth and thus reducing the number of well-paying jobs.

In short, the 2016 election fractured the vote of the economically disadvantaged along lines of race and ethnicity. While the rhetoric and appeals of the campaign were particularly strident and frequently appalling, there is actually a high level of continuity between the 2016 election and the previous fifty years of electoral history. *As in every presidential election since 1964*, the Democratic presidential candidate won large majorities of the vote among racial and ethnic minorities, and the Republican won a majority among the more numerous white population. Moreover, Democratic strength among whites in 2016 was the weakest among those who had ended their formal education at or before high school graduation.

Seen in this light, the 2016 election was simply the most recent installment in the past fifty years of presidential elections in which the Democratic Party has been unable to win majority support within the white population. Just as important, the party's appeal among whites during this period became increasingly focused toward those who are better educated and politically liberal. These emergent patterns of support stand in sharp and dramatic contrast to the historical patterns of both parties' respective bases of support.

The modern Democratic Party was born in the depths of the Great Depression during the 1930s, and it revolutionized American politics by becoming the champion of the white working class and an ardent supporter of labor unions. At the same time, it continued to depend on the solid support of the South, and hence accomplished little in the way of dramatic policy change aimed at the direct benefit of African Americans until the late 1940s. During the subsequent half-century, Democrats became the champions of civil rights for African Americans, while also becoming increasingly dependent on the votes of both well-educated whites and ethnic and racial minorities. At the same time, they were becoming less successful at securing the votes of the white working class.

In contrast, the Republican Party came into being during the crisis of secession, the Civil War, and the postwar effort during Reconstruction (Foner 1988, 2005, 2010). Moreover, to the extent that Reconstruction was successful, it was due to the strong support of the Republican Party in the post–Civil War Congress. Indeed, the Thirteenth, Fourteenth, and Fifteenth Amendments were entirely due to the support and leadership of the Republican Party. Hence, African Americans became stalwart supporters of the Republican Party – the party that also represented the interests of eastern business and industry. While such a coalition may seem incongruous, it is helpful to remember that Abraham Lincoln's law practice was actively engaged by the primary industry of his day – the railroads – and his political roots were nurtured in a Whig Party that supported "internal improvements" and encouraged industrial development.

Republicans continued to carry the mantle of civil rights leadership throughout the early part of the twentieth century, particularly in the period prior to the civil rights transformation of the Democratic Party that began during the New Deal (Schickler 2016). Indeed, successfully passing landmark civil rights legislation in the 1950s and 1960s depended on crucial Republican support and leadership (Whalen and Whalen 1985). By the end of this period, however, a transformed Republican Party had come to embrace the doctrines of property rights and states' rights – positions that won the continuing support of its conservative wing as well as leading to the conversion of the South from being solidly Democratic to becoming the central and most reliable element in the new Republican coalition. A central actor in this transformational drama was Senator Strom Thurmond of South Carolina, who not only led the Dixiecrat defection from the Democratic Party in 1948 but also converted to the Republican Party and led Barry Goldwater's effort to capture the southern vote in 1964 (Crespino 2012).

In summary, voters in the 2016 presidential election were the inheritors of an electorate and a political system that had experienced a political inversion since the end of World War II. The party of Lincoln and black emancipation had become the party of white southerners and white working-class rebellion. The Democratic Party, which had been based on the support of the white working class, had become the party of civil rights, racial and ethnic minorities, and well-educated liberals – most of whom were whites. The political implications of this inversion are both profound and crucial to understanding not only contemporary American politics but also the evolution of social welfare policy.

First, the political views of the American working class are deeply divided, particularly along lines of race and ethnicity. White working-class supporters of Donald Trump and the Republican Party are typically skeptical of government programs aimed at ameliorating the challenges faced by the less affluent, even though they are likely to be primary beneficiaries of many such programs (Achen and Bartels 2016; Bartels 2008). Together with more affluent and conservative whites, they provide the backbone of support for the Republican Party and the primary opposition to any extension of social welfare benefits.

Second, and at the same time, the labor unions that have tradition-ally supplied the primary organizational impetus behind working-class politics and the extension of social welfare benefits have withered in size and declined in influence, owing not only to the migration of manu-facturing to foreign labor markets but also the migration of American manufacturing to southern states hostile to labor union organization. Even though the Volkswagen Corporation supported the United Auto Workers' effort aimed at organizing workers at its Chattanooga plant, the plant's workers narrowly voted against union representation after a concerted and highly politicized effort by prominent political leaders in Tennessee aimed at stopping the effort (Greenhouse 2014).

Third, the affluent middle class is divided in its political loyalties as well, primarily along lines of political ideology. One part is aligned with traditionally conservative, Republican-inspired views favoring small government and individual initiative, typically endorsing conservative social and political values. Another element aligns with the Democratic Party, supporting extensions of a social welfare state and favoring more liberal social and political values and policies.

THE DEPARTURE OF THE SOUTH AS A PIVOT POINT

The unstable political arrangement that made the social and economic programs of the New Deal possible was undone by the response of a southern backlash to the use of the Fourteenth Amendment's equal pro-tection clause in the furtherance of civil rights and voting rights. The so-called Southern Manifesto of 1956 was issued as a "Declaration of Constitutional Principles" in response to the Supreme Court's 1954 Brown desegregation decision. Its signatories were nineteen sena-tors and eighty-two House members (ninety-nine Democrats and two Republicans) – all of whom were from the states of the old confederacy. They gave voice to the southern delegation's continuing opposition to the civil rights agenda, defending states' rights and disputing the role of the Supreme Court in its use of the Fourteenth Amendment to insure equal (color-blind) treatment of citizens by the states.

Exceptions to this pattern of support among the supporters and nonsupporters are notable. Three southern senators failed to sign the manifesto – Lyndon Johnson from Texas as well as Estes Kefauver and Albert Gore, both from Tennessee. All three senators nurtured their own national political aspirations, and they represented states not typically identified as part of the Deep South. Just as important, they came from states with relatively smaller concentrations of African American residents. The nonsigners in the House also came from states outside the traditional Deep South with smaller African American population concentrations: Texas, Tennessee, Florida, and North Carolina.

At the same time, the signers *included* Democratic senators and House members who had been stalwart supporters of social welfare legislation. The Alabama congressional delegation, for example, included members of the Big Jim Folsom populist faction of the Democratic Party (Key 1949). Alabama senators Lister Hill and John Sparkman, as well as several House members, had been Folsom-inspired populists and strong supporters of social welfare legislation. Like many other southern supporters of populism and the New Deal, however, they inevitably failed to avoid the trip wire of racially charged politics and hence embraced white supremacy.

This event, in which Republicans were virtually absent from the manifesto's list of supporters, represents one of the final moments of strong Republican support for civil rights. Supreme Court chief justice Earl Warren, who wrote the majority opinion in the *Brown* case, was new to the court after a distinguished career as a Republican politician and governor of California. The Republican president Dwight Eisenhower appointed Warren to the court and sent troops to enforce the *Brown* decision at Central High School in Little Rock, even though he privately disapproved of the court's decision in the case (Leuchtenburg 2015). At this particular political moment in time, one might well have thought that the forces in support of civil rights were perhaps becoming ascendant, with strong support from Republicans as well as rapidly developing support among nonsouthern Democrats (Douglas 1971; Humphrey 1976; Schickler 2016; Schickler, Pearson, and Feinstein 2010).

Such an assumption would soon have been demonstrated to be false. Over time, formerly liberal southern Democrats who had supported the New Deal social welfare programs not only opposed the equal treatment of African Americans but many began to embrace more generally conservative positions on social and economic legislation. Southern support for social welfare legislation began to evaporate when the benefits were extended to blacks as well as whites. Hence, the economically liberal and populist southern politicians who had provided bedrock support for liberal New Deal social legislation became an endangered species in the New South, as a consequence of *both* replacement *and* conversion.

Ultimately, even moderate and conservative Democrats became part of an increasingly endangered species in southern elections. While

Barry Goldwater and Strom Thurmond led the way for the migration of southern Democrats to the Republican Party in 1964 (Crespino 2012), the movement was embraced and extended by the southern strategy of Richard Nixon in 1968. As with many other Republicans of the time, Nixon had previously cultivated his own credentials as a supporter of civil rights, only to jettison that history by moving to embrace a southern strategy aimed at white southerners disenchanted by the direction of the national Democratic Party.

In this context, the earlier depth of Republican support for African American civil rights can be easily overstated. With the *Brown* case pending, Eisenhower invited Chief Justice Warren to a White House dinner where John W. Davis, the attorney for the segregationists, was also present. In a private moment, Eisenhower shared his thoughts with Warren: "These are not bad people. All they are concerned about is to see that their sweet little girls are not required to sit in school alongside some big overgrown Negroes" (Leuchtenburg 2015: 361). Eisenhower's comments failed to sway the chief justice, but they demonstrate that Republican support for civil rights was sometimes deeply felt, often politically convenient, and at other times wholly expendable. The best that can be said regarding Eisenhower and the *Brown* decision was that he publicly supported the court and its ruling, thereby avoiding a constitutional crisis, even though he deeply disagreed with the decision.

The migration to the Republican Party moved rapidly in the South, thus transforming the base of the party (Black and Black 2002). By the end of the 1990s, southern Republicans occupied the speakership of the House of Representatives, the role of Republican majority leader in the Senate, and the chairmanship of the national Republican Party. Hence, in relatively short order, the South went from being the pivot point for the political successes of the New Deal to becoming the pivot point for the successes of the new Republican Party ushered into American politics by Strom Thurmond, Barry Goldwater, and Richard Nixon.

The result has not been simply a southern phenomenon, however. Again, the Democratic Party's presidential candidate has failed to obtain a majority among white voters for the past half-century – not since the 1964 presidential election of Lyndon Johnson, which occurred in the traumatic aftermath of the Kennedy assassination. Moreover, while the Democratic Party thus depends on obtaining support among non-whites, it has not been as successful among Latino Americans and Asian Americans as it has been among African Americans. Indeed, as party coalitions in America transform from being biracial to multiracial, new problems arise in addressing the common challenges to social, political, and economic inequality that have been the self-declared mission of liberal and progressive movements in American politics (Schickler 2016).

These political processes played out in a larger economic context characterized by a rise in economic inequality and a continuing concentration of wealth, not only in the United States (Bartels 2008; Piketty and Saez 2003) but internationally as well (Piketty 2014). Indeed, America has been characterized as a political and economic order that is driven by, what might be called, an oligarchy of the rich (Gilens 2014; Gilens and Page 2014; Hacker and Pierson 2010; Winters and Page 2009). In this context, the emergence of cross-national oligarchic collusion that has recently become a prominent issue in relations between the United States and Russia is symptomatic of ongoing political transformations *within* domestic political arrangements. Democrats and Republicans compete for support among the elements of this oligarchy, with candidates of both parties relying on a donor class that includes the titans of Wall Street.

THE PERNICIOUS REALIGNMENT

In advancing the cause of fundamental civil rights and voting rights, the lines of political competition between the two major American political parties have been redrawn in a way that creates disadvantages for the larger American working class across all racial groups – blacks, whites, Latino Americans, and Asian Americans. During the 1930s and 1940s, the Democratic Party's New Deal coalition came to represent those working-class interests in ways that were new to American politics. These historical efforts produced dramatic advances in the creation of the framework for a social welfare state – the Fair Labor Standards Act, the Social Security Act, and a variety of economic planning and employment relief programs. The enduring problem was that this progress was based on a fundamentally compromised and ultimately self-defeating political arrangement. The New Deal could succeed only if it maintained the support of the solidly Democratic congressional delegations of the American South. And such support could only be secured if white supremacy and racial apartheid in the South were allowed to continue (Katznelson 2013).

Multiple symptoms of these enduring problems continue to be apparent. First, the racial tensions within the Democratic Party's working class base have never disappeared, particularly in the South but in other parts of the country as well. While many Americans have been proud to call the United States a nation of immigrants, the experience has never been without its share of conflict, and resistance to new arrivals spreads far beyond the South, from the Atlantic to the Pacific Seaboards.

Second, the hostility to new arrivals accelerated as non-European flows of immigrants increased. As Hofstadter (1955) documented early on, the roots of the Progressive movement in America during the late nineteenth and early twentieth centuries were anchored in the efforts of the middle class to defend its political and economic positions relative to the challenges of rapid industrialization and newly arriving immigrant streams. California provides an excellent case study (Mowry 1951). As in other regions of the country, the state's Progressive movement was anchored in efforts of the middle class to defend its political and economic positions relative to both the captains of industry – particularly the railroad barons – and the new immigrants who were arriving from China, Mexico, the Philippines, and other parts of the United States. Neither the captains of industry nor the California Progressive movement, which was primarily located in the California Republican Party, was particularly sympathetic to the concerns of these lower economic classes.

Fifty years later, at the same time that the Congress was on the verge of passing historic civil rights and voting rights legislation, the California legislature passed, and Democratic governor Pat Brown signed, the 1963 Rumford Fair Housing Act, prohibiting racial discrimination in the sale and rental of residential property. In response, California citizens rose up in self-righteous indignation to enact Ballot Proposition 14 that repealed the Rumford Act in 1964. Two years later Governor Pat Brown was defeated in his 1966 reelection bid by Ronald Reagan, the conservative Republican candidate who supported the repeal. In short, the Rumford Act and Proposition 14 drove a race-based wedge into the predominantly working-class coalition of the California Democratic Party, defeating a popular governor and leading to a conservative rejuvenation of the Republican Party in California politics.

At the same time that California's Republican Party was rejuvenated, it was also being realigned and redefined. Conservative Senate Republicans like S. I. Hayakawa and George Murphy would ultimately replace moderate Republicans, such as US senator Thomas Kuchel – a strong supporter of civil rights. And the liberally inclined Republican Party that elected Earl Warren as governor would ultimately nominate and elect Ronald Reagan. In New York State, liberal Republicans, such as Senator Jacob Javits and Governor Nelson Rockefeller, would be replaced by conservative Republicans as well.

Similar patterns were occurring in other states, making it difficult for moderate Republicans to survive in electoral politics. In Nebraska, the politically moderate Republican governor Norbert Tiemann was turned out of office in favor of the conservative Democrat and future senator J. James Exxon. The brand of Republicanism represented by Oregon's former senator and governor Mark Hatfield – who combined evangelical religion, opposition to the Vietnam War, and support for civil rights – was quickly becoming a historical artifact. In short, the ideological complexion of the Republican Party was rapidly changing across the nation, with Republicans repositioning themselves at more conservative positions across a broad range of issues, including social welfare spending, civil liberties, and civil rights.

Third, the American working class disproportionately reflects the racial and ethnic heterogeneity of the American population. This heterogeneity has made it difficult to sustain a political movement that depends on social homogeneity to construct a politically self-conscious working-class identity. Hence, it also becomes increasingly difficult to construct a collective identity supporting unified working-class interests. Crucial progress in the furtherance of civil rights for all Americans has created political resistance within a racially and ethnically fragmented working class, thus standing in the way of further progress.

Fourth, the American political culture has not been sympathetic to a self-conscious working-class identification. In an environment where social mobility is a widely held goal, and middle-class membership is highly regarded, working-class loyalties and self-identifications are difficult to sustain, even in the absence of racial and ethnic divisions within the working class. In short, working-class consciousness has not been easily reconciled with prevailing elements of both popular and political cultures, as well as within the racial and ethnic divisions among the working-class population.

Finally, growing working-class resentment toward the rising proportion of well-educated Americans is nearly inevitable. As we will see, the rise of the educated class of professional and managerial individuals has produced several consequences. First, a substantial proportion of the population that is well compensated and well educated is also sheltered from many of the social and economic challenges facing the American working class. Second, this well-educated class of Americans has become a central component of the Democratic Party coalition, thereby shifting the focus of the party away from its former core constituency – the American working class.

Indeed, the demographic rise of the educated class in American life plays a significant role in accounting for economic inequality. A major factor in explaining the economic rise of the top 1 percent's share of national income revolves around the rise of this highly educated, well-compensated sector of American society. The membership of this group is not only composed of the captains of industry but also an increasing number of professionals who command high salaries in the medical, legal, technology, and financial sectors (Piketty and Saez 2003; Rothwell 2017).

LONG-TERM ECONOMIC TRANSFORMATION

Long-term economic trends have, in short, created obstacles for the political influence of the working-class population, with continuing erosion in the availability of well-paid manufacturing jobs in the United States and elsewhere. Not coincidentally, American labor unions are in retreat, both in the declining proportion of the labor force they represent and in their declining influence in the policy-making process. These same labor unions were at the forefront of the civil rights movement in American politics, and their decline has created a social as well as an economic vacuum in the American political process.

In short, the extensions of civil rights and voting rights have not erased the problems of poverty, underemployment, and inequality. Instead, these problems have been institutionalized within particularly vulnerable populations. Rather than uniting and expanding the working class as a political movement, we have seen a long-term decline in the political strength and cohesiveness of the working class as well as the decline of organized labor. Hence, it is difficult to ignore the fact that political, social, and economic equality continue to erode in American society, at a moment when the primary beneficiaries are themselves deeply divided over social welfare legislation.

Moreover, vast financial resources are becoming increasingly concentrated within an even smaller percentage of the society – a group much smaller than the well-compensated professional classes. Thus, a political, as well as an economic oligarchy, is on the rise, not only in the United States but in other advanced industrial nations as well (Gilens 2014; Gilens and Page 2014; Winters and Page 2009). A long and respected pluralist tradition in political science (see Dahl 1961) encourages skepticism regarding correlations between wealth and political influence, suggesting that wealth does not immediately translate into political influence. Such skepticism warrants reconsideration, particularly when free speech is defined in the context of campaign contributions (*Citizens United* v. *FEC*).

Forbes Magazine produces an annual list of the world's richest people, and its 2017 list includes 2043 billionaires, with an average net worth of $3.75 billion (www.forbes.com/billionaires). Donald Trump was on the list, ranked at number 544, with a net worth of $3.5 billion, placing him within the upper reaches of the second quartile within the overall distribution. The rank order of billionaires per country for the top five countries is the United States (565), China (319), Germany (114), India (101), and Russia (96). The state of California has 140, which would put it in third place if listed as a separate country.

The concentration of wealth does not provide definitive evidence of political oligarchy, and indeed, the level of oligarchy varies quite dramatically across the five countries with the most billionaires. Rather, a political economy marked by extreme wealth in the context of large impoverished populations raises the question of the vitality and performance of democratic institutions. Russia and China certainly rank highly on the list of suspect cases. Still, in the context of the United States, the following question arises: How can it be that, during a long post–World War II era of increasing prosperity and economic growth, the concentration of resources has increasingly been enhanced within an economic elite while so many Americans have been left behind? Our argument is that the political structure of American political parties has given rise to political institutions that are failing to create a political economy that sustains the broadly based social and economic well-being of all Americans.

PROBLEMS IN MAINTAINING THE GREAT TRADE-OFF

More than forty years ago, Arthur Okun (1975) discussed the great trade-off in democratic politics between equality and efficiency. Both are crucial, he argued, to the health of democracy. Absent equality, democracy is undermined. Absent economic efficiency, a society cannot generate the level of prosperity necessary for the creation and maintenance of even modest levels of economic equality. The problem arises when one is pursued at the permanent expense of the other, thereby undermining the great trade-off necessary to sustain both.

According to this view, democratic politics works most effectively when it forces a grand compromise between parties and politics that take both goals seriously – a grand compromise that has been historically vulnerable to political manipulation (Tufte 1978). Unfortunately, American politics and political coalitions have evolved in a way that does not adequately represent either set of interests. Neither an exclusive focus on equality nor an exclusive focus on efficiency is likely to sustain a successfully stable equilibrium (Huckfeldt and Kohfeld 1989). In contemporary American politics, neither oligarchy nor a working-class political movement fractured by racial and ethnic division is likely to make progress in achieving either equality or efficiency within the American economy and the American political process. Indeed, the primary solution to oligarchic domination is a healthy system of party competition that includes the political representation of working-class and lower-middle-class interests – interests defined in terms of social welfare and economic grievance rather than cultural grievance and racial hostility.

As a combined consequence, and regardless of rising economic inequality among Americans (Bartels 2008; Gilens 2014; Piketty 2014), a shrinking proportion of the population identifies as working class. In deference perhaps to an egalitarian instinct, vast majorities identify as members of the middle class. Correspondingly, when liberal politicians make class-based appeals to their constituencies, they typically reach out to this vaguely defined middle class. At the same time, if we conceive the middle class in terms of a comfortable lifestyle, a healthy savings account, modest levels of economic security, and the capacity to put their children through college, an increasingly large proportion of the American population fails to qualify.

Hence, the amorphous and misleading picture of a burgeoning middle class fails to acknowledge that a substantial proportion of the American population either aspires to membership but fails to achieve it or achieves membership with only the most tenuous grasp. While one might wish that everyone in America achieved middle class status, wishing does not make it so, and even the economic vitality of middle-income – or median-income – Americans faces severe challenges. As a consequence, definitions of shared economic circumstance are rarely invoked as a motivating theme in contemporary American politics. And when invoked, they are often employed by economically conservative populists opposed to racial and ethnic pluralism.

SOCIAL WELFARE AND THE COLLISION OF CLASS, RACE, AND ETHNICITY

In 1905, Werner Sombart famously asked the following question: Why is there no socialism in the United States? He offered a long list of explanations, but the one factor that best maintains its relevance is the failure to accommodate racial and ethnic diversity within the working-class population. This failure carries profound implications for parties at both ends of the ideological spectrum. In the pages that follow, we consider the failures of the American welfare state in the context of Sombart's diagnosis.

In Okun's terms, we might expect Republicans to be the party of efficiency, and Democrats to be the party of economic equality, yet neither party has adequately articulated these agendas. The Democratic Party often conflates ethnicity and race with economic standing, but indeed concerns related to class are not entirely subsumed by those related to race and ethnicity, and neither does class subsume race and ethnicity. Similarly, the Republican Party tends to conflate issues related to efficiency not only with economically conservative principles that would help to conserve a market economy but with socially conservative principles as well. And many of these socially conservative principles conflict with market realities. The economic backlash to the North Carolina Republican Party's socially conservative policies has been centered in some of the state's most vital economic enterprises, and similar responses have occurred in other red states, including the repudiation of Governor Sam Brownback's "Kansas experiment." In short, there is a substantial body of evidence to suggest that the current structure of partisan institutions in American politics is poorly designed to accomplish *either* equality *or* efficiency.

3

Civil Rights, Social Welfare, and Populism

As the civil rights movement began to take shape, with integration of schools as a primary focus, segregationists realized that the end of "separate but equal" school systems was coming soon, which meant that any federal aid to white school children would include federal aid to black school children as well. The segregationists were perfectly willing to sacrifice the futures of millions of poor white children to make sure the blacks were held down.

—Congressman Carl Elliott, Alabama
(Elliott and D'Orso 1992: 129)

The populist impulse in American politics is to level the playing field in both politics and the economy. Leveling the playing field in politics means creating a political process that reflects the "one person, one vote" democratic ethos – a politics in which every vote counts and influence is not a simple by-product of wealth, birth, or social standing. Leveling the field in economic terms takes on a variety of meanings, from (1) dramatic attempts at income redistribution to (2) more modest efforts at creating a social welfare state that provides some basic level of social welfare services in the areas of health, housing, nutrition, and education that are available for all to (3) creating high barriers to immigration and trade aimed at keeping jobs in America for Americans. Hence, populist appeals take on a variety of forms, from progressive to regressive, and each must be judged relative to its own context and content.

At its best, the populist instinct reflects a commitment to Lincoln's vision of a government that is "of the people, by the people and for the people." At the same time, such a "progressive" populist impulse has been historically vulnerable to being sidetracked and manipulated by the misleading claims of opportunistic elites who claim to be the champions of everyday citizens. Acting on the populist impulse requires a significant level of political information and expertise on the part of citizens to ascertain the political institutions, processes, candidates, and policies that benefit the common citizen and the common purpose. Examples of misleading populist appeals have been common throughout American history, as well as in contemporary times.

The South has been justifiably famous for its historically abundant supply of populist politicians. Some of these, like Governor "Big Jim" Folsom of Alabama, were by most accounts *progressive* populists motivated to represent the common ordinary (white) citizen, and at times reached out to black citizens as well. Others, like Theodore Bilbo of Mississippi, were purveyors of a *regressive* populism and the shameless manipulators of white fears and prejudices regarding both the elites and African Americans (Key 1949; Woodward 1955). Still others, such as Hubert Humphrey of Minnesota, have been progressive populists who embraced civil rights, unions, and social welfare measures on behalf of the disadvantaged. In his own words, "The moral test of government is how it treats those who are in the dawn of life, the children; those who are in the twilight of life, the aged; and those in the shadows of life, the sick, the needy and the handicapped" (Congressional Record, November 4, 1977). In short, the populist label covers a broad range of politicians and policies, and we leave it to the readers to make their own judgments regarding constructive and unscrupulous populist politicians in American politics, but the veracity of populist leadership clearly warrants careful scrutiny.

Indeed, a common technique in the arsenal of politicians who claim the cloak of populism has been to identify not only the elite opponents of the common citizen but also the socially marginal citizens defined as threats to the supposedly worthy citizen (Kazin 1998). Hence, populism in Nazi Germany identified Jewish citizens as the source of all danger, while southern demagogues stigmatized African Americans as the enemy. The important point is that the populist impulse is neither uniformly beneficial nor uniformly pernicious. Rather, like many political impulses, it is vulnerable to manipulation, and such manipulation is particularly likely in the context of poorly informed citizens (Achen and Bartels 2016).

Many observers have reflexively associated populism with the fascism of Europe prior to World War II and with other right-wing, antidemocratic movements. It would be a disservice to democratic politics to label all populist appeals as manipulative efforts at misleading the voters or as uniformly conservative. Consider the following excerpt from Franklin Roosevelt's speech at Madison Square Garden several days before his first reelection victory in 1936.

We have not come this far without a struggle and I assure you we cannot go further without a struggle.

For twelve years this Nation was afflicted with hear-nothing, see-nothing, do-nothing Government. The Nation looked to Government but the Government looked away.... Powerful influences strive today to restore that kind of government with its doctrine that that Government is best which is most indifferent.

For nearly four years you have had an Administration which instead of twirling its thumbs has rolled up its sleeves. We will keep our sleeves rolled up.

We had to struggle with the old enemies of peace – business and financial monopoly, speculation, reckless banking, class antagonism, sectionalism, war profiteering.

They had begun to consider the Government of the United States as a mere appendage to their own affairs. We know now that Government by organized money is just as dangerous as Government by organized mob.

Never before in all our history have these forces been so united against one candidate as they stand today. They are unanimous in their hate for me – and I welcome their hatred.

I should like to have it said of my first Administration that in it the forces of selfishness and of lust for power met their match. I should like to have it said of my second Administration that in it these forces met their master.

These were strong words with an explicitly populist appeal. While some would consider the speech to be an unfair attack aimed at manipulating the public, many others have viewed the speech as a compelling attack on corporate greed and oligarchic control. Populist appeals, like all political appeals, must pass the test of public scrutiny and criticism. Indeed, several different sources of legitimate opposition confront the populist impulse. Perhaps most importantly, the well-being of all citizens depends on economic growth, and thus reasonable concerns arise over the impact of populism on economic health and vitality. This is, indeed, the central trade-off that Okun (1975) identified and we discussed in Chapter 2. Even though one might, for example, value equality more than efficiency, Okun argued quite effectively that equality and efficiency are interdependent, and hence, progress in achieving equality depends on efficiency gains that lead to economic growth.

In Okun's view, the goal of social and economic policy was to reach this balance between equality and efficiency, and the job of policy makers and economic advisers was to fine-tune taxing and spending to maintain an equilibrium that maximized both. The problem is that in the intervening forty years, there has been a rapid growth in inequality that serves to undermine this great trade-off. Between now and the time that Okun was writing, the share of the national income going to the richest 1 percent has increased from 8 percent to 20 percent (Summers 2015a). If the income distribution reverted to 1979 levels, the income of the bottom 80 percent would increase by nearly 25 percent, and the income of the top 1 percent would be reduced by 50 percent (Summers 2015b). Using still a different measure, the ratio of within-firm compensation of CEOs to average workers within the same firms went from 20 to 1 in 1965 to 295.9 to 1 in 2013 (Mishel and Davis 2014).

Thus, in contemporary circumstances, tinkering with the current balance between equality and efficiency falls short, and the case for major redistribution looms large. Such an extreme maldistribution of resources may indeed justify a call for a populist response in the tradition of Roosevelt's New Deal. Quite clearly, however, the contemporary political system is not well equipped to respond to such a call.

GROUP CONFLICT OVER SOCIAL WELFARE

An entirely separate challenge to social welfare policy arises due to group resentments and hostility. Some of these resentments are class-based – a substantial proportion of the affluent classes resents any effort aimed at taxing their incomes in the interests of the less affluent. Another set of resentments arises *among* the potential recipients of the benefits, typically as a consequence of ethnic and racial competition, suspicion, or hostility. The quotation from Alabama congressman Carl Elliott introducing this chapter reflects the hostilities arising among the potential recipients of social welfare benefits in the South during the 1950s. Elliott's statement identifies a core problem confronted not only by populist congressmen from the South who wished to support social welfare legislation on behalf of their disadvantaged constituents during the 1950s but also for earlier efforts by the New Deal Democratic Party as well as subsequent and contemporary efforts by social welfare advocates more generally.

Elliott represented a hill country district in northern Alabama from 1949 to 1965, and he built his House career on strong support for social welfare legislation serving the interests of the rural and small town constituencies that he served – constituencies that were largely white and impoverished. In addition to being the floor leader for the National Defense Education Act of 1958 that provided the first federal support for elementary and secondary education, he was a strong supporter of a broad range of social welfare legislation. Indeed, he was recognized as a leading southern liberal and ultimately received the first "Profiles in Courage Award" from the Kennedy Center.

His support for social welfare legislation was possible among his white Alabama constituents because they saw it as being in their own interests. While he was not a Bilbo-style race baiter, he signed the Southern Manifesto, advocated the "gradualist approach" to civil rights, voted against the 1964 Civil Rights Act (CRA), and tread softly on issues that might inflame the racial hostility of his constituents. While issues regarding race were relatively remote to his immediate constituency, they were not remote to his state, and he ultimately lost his seat when he came into conflict with George Wallace and the hard-core segregationists.

As Key's earlier work (1949) made clear, the populist faction in Alabama politics thrived in the predominantly poor white areas of the state. Like other Alabama populists, Elliott's career and his constituency were not immune to the issues that inflamed racial hostility within the state, even though African Americans were not part of his congressional district constituency. Hence, his support for social welfare legislation was contingent on his ability to separate support for social welfare legislation from the toxic racial environment that permeated not only the politics of Alabama and the rest of the South but many other areas of the country as well.

GROUP CONFLICT AND SOCIAL WELFARE
IN A FEDERAL CONTEXT

The anxieties and hostilities of racial politics have presented similar obstacles to the ambitions and goals of many national efforts that have attempted to represent the interests of the disadvantaged. Franklin Roosevelt and his New Deal attempted to avoid many of these problems by being cautious and circumspect on issues of race and by funneling most New Deal programs through the states. In this way, social welfare for the white population was kept separate from issues that might threaten white dominance, and the New Deal was not, in general, perceived as a threat to white racial hegemony.

This strategy was at times bypassed by lower-profile programs administered directly from the White House by Harry Hopkins on a racially neutral basis (Holmes 1972), a strategy subsequently reflected in some War on Poverty programs during the Johnson administration. This strategy created other political problems, however. The Great Society Programs of the Johnson administration produced a firestorm of criticism among state and local government officials who welcomed the funds but objected to the national government's constraints on their use.

Complaints such as these ultimately led to not only a variety of block grant and revenue-sharing programs with more flexibility at the state and local levels but also less national government control over targeting the support to particular beneficiaries. Hence, local control often sacrificed community development, neighborhood rejuvenation, and poverty programs to efforts focused on economic development. Rather than funneling federal aid to poverty-impacted areas, general revenue sharing and community development block grant programs spread the aid as widely as possible and to as many jurisdictions as possible. Such a decentralization initiative was especially popular among Republican office holders. During the Nixon administration's years of budgetary surpluses, these programs became popular among many recipient governments, but when the budget surpluses disappeared, so did the programs (Donovan 1967; Judd 1979).

THE FOCUS ON SOCIAL WELFARE

Problems related to economic rather than political inequality were certainly recognized by Martin Luther King Jr. and others within the civil rights movement. At the end of his life, King was looking beyond issues of political inequality to address issues surrounding poverty, and he created his Poor People's Campaign organized around the goal of uniting the poor of all racial groups to address problems of poverty. He was, indeed, planning a poor people's march on Washington, DC, at the time of his 1968 assassination in Memphis, and he had come to Memphis to assist in a strike by the sanitation workers.

The issues that confront African Americans and other racial and ethnic minorities are related to not only the denial of full citizenship, due process, and equal protection but also the absence of a political movement or political party that unites disadvantaged citizens of all races and ethnicities in support of social welfare programs. The central problem in creating such a movement frequently involves conflict and hostilities based on race and ethnicity among the likely recipients. The civil rights movement received support both among minorities and among liberal whites, but most liberal whites were middle-class individuals, more easily motivated by the denial of political and citizenship rights rather than furtherance of economic rights.

This has created deep divisions among Democratic Party constituencies. Traditional New Deal constituencies, such as the labor movement, were motivated primarily by economic distress, and some (but not all) American labor unions were at the forefront of the civil rights movement in American politics. While the strong advocacy of civil rights attracted many liberal affluent whites to support the Democratic Party, economic issues related to poverty and class were typically less compelling, and support for programs aimed at economic equality would prove to be broadly unpopular even among many relatively disadvantaged white citizens. To paraphrase Congressman Elliott, many white citizens were unwilling to support programs that benefitted racial minorities, even at the price of sacrificing the well-being of poor whites.

The success of the civil rights movement, focused primarily on equal political rights for minorities, not only exposed the tension between the northern and southern Democrats but also led to a full-scale realignment of the political parties. As long as the liberal agenda was defined in terms of support for social welfare legislation primarily administered through state governments, the solid Democratic South was an active and crucial participant in the creation of social welfare legislation. The movement of African Americans out of the South – particularly to cities in the North and West – ultimately put an end to this political arrangement.

Indeed, the "Great Migration" of African Americans out of the South would be crucial in transforming the politics of the entire nation. First, many northerners were, at least initially, more sympathetic to the plight of African Americans and less hostile to their presence in the northern states. Second, African American voters in major American cities became an important resource to Democratic Party organizations across the North. Democratic Party supporters of civil rights – such as Hubert Humphrey in Minnesota and Paul Douglas in Illinois – began to win elections in the northern states. This led to substantial progress in the furtherance of a civil rights agenda, and ultimately to success in the furtherance of a social welfare agenda. At the same time, Democratic progress on the civil rights agenda meant that southern Democrats began to leave the party and forsake its candidates. Moreover, northern cities offered no panacea to problems of racial animosity, and the civil rights agenda would ultimately become less popular in the North as well.

THE 1948 ELECTION AS A PIVOT POINT

Within this context, the 1948 election was a crucial turning point in the history of race relations, the Democratic Party, and the nation. In that year, two Democrats would be newly elected to the US Senate: Hubert Humphrey, a former pharmacist and mayor of Minneapolis, and Paul Douglas, a University of Chicago economist, former Chicago alderman, and former president of the American Economic Association. Both had been nominated but not yet elected to their new Senate seats at the time of the Democratic national party convention, and both played prominent roles in the adoption of the civil rights plank to the party platform – the plank that led ultimately to Strom Thurmond's presidential candidacy and the Dixiecrat revolt. Indeed, Humphrey gave the dramatic convention speech in support of the civil rights plank that mobilized the party and also led to the southern walkout. The civil rights support of Humphrey and Douglas stood out among their new colleagues, and they established the paradigm for the northern, liberal, pro-civil rights senator. Their own autobiographical accounts, published at the end of their careers, provide insight on these crucial moments in the development of the civil rights agenda (Humphrey 1976; Douglas 1971).

President Harry Truman had previously established the President's Committee on Civil Rights in 1946 – a presidential commission that submitted its findings to Truman in December 1947. Its recommendations included the establishment of a permanent Civil Rights Commission, a Joint Congressional Committee on Rights, and a Civil Rights Division in the Department of Justice. The Democratic convention took place in mid-July 1948, and later in the same month Truman ordered the desegregation of both the armed services and the federal civilian workforce. In short, Truman's actions in combination with the party's convention set a new path for the Democratic Party that was a turning point in American politics.

The result would be a political realignment that (1) ultimately made the Democratic Party the party of civil rights as well as (2) created a new South that was nearly as solidly Republican as the old South had been solidly Democratic (Carmines and Stimson 1981, 1989). The changes did not stop there, however. As the Republican Party became more conservative on both social welfare issues and on civil rights issues, liberal Republican voters would ultimately leave the party. As a consequence, important cascading changes also occurred in the ideological and partisan makeup of other regions within the country, reflected by the partisanship and voting records of their congressional representatives. Southern Democrats had been some of the most important social welfare liberals of their day, just as today southern Republicans have become the outstanding champions of social welfare conservatism. In contrast, not only have Northeastern and West Coast moderate Republicans become an endangered species but West Coast, Midwest, and Northeast Democrats have also become increasingly liberal. Indeed, this ideological polarization between the congressional parties dramatically increased as a consequence of the 2018 midterm elections, and it is likely to increase further as a consequence of the 2020 general election.

The resulting realignment of the parties was not *only* a matter of Democrats replacing Republicans and vice versa. Individual members of Congress altered their ideological loyalties and political positions on social welfare legislation. As the civil rights movement gained momentum, southern Democrats ran for cover, becoming increasingly conservative on both social welfare issues and racial issues before ultimately being replaced by conservative Republicans. At the same time, many northern Democrats – compelled by the influence of the civil rights cause – became increasingly liberal. John Kennedy, for example, had been a moderate on civil rights issues before adjusting his position after becoming president. Indeed, the earliest progress on civil rights during the modern period – passing the 1957 and 1964 Civil Rights Acts – was only possible due to the strong support among northern Republicans.

In the aftermath of the great civil rights victories of the 1960s, the Democratic Party became, quite paradoxically, a less effective advocate for the disadvantaged. Not only did the Democrats lose the South and its strong support for social welfare legislation but their support among the white working class was compromised as well (Abramson, Aldrich, and Rohde 2002; Huckfeldt and Kohfeld 1989), at the same time that labor unions declined as a potent force in national politics.

THE GREAT MIGRATION, WORLD WAR II, AND
THE REVOLUTION IN CIVIL RIGHTS

The success of the civil rights revolution can be more fully understood in terms of the long-term political implications of two significant events. First, the "Great Migration" of African Americans out of the South redirected the future of American politics. Slavery and its aftermath created a political culture in the South that was far different from the political culture of northern cities. Cities in the North – New York, Chicago, Detroit, Philadelphia, Cleveland, and so on – had developed long-standing practices regarding the political incorporation of new arrivals. Indeed, these newcomers provided the historical backbone of many urban political organizations, both Republican and Democratic. A standard practice based on securing political advantage was to mobilize the votes of new arrivals. Hence, when a substantial population of African Americans arrived in northern cities, political leaders saw them as a potential resource, and their presence changed the political calculus of state and local party organizations.

The Great Migration of African Americans out of the South and into northern cities began during the economically prosperous times of the 1920s, slowed during the Great Depression, but was then renewed in the 1940s as a consequence of employment opportunities related to war industries. For example, Oakland and its busy port became a destination for many African Americans seeking employment during World War II. And the employment of African Americans was made possible when Roosevelt signed an executive order requiring an end to racial discrimination in war industries.

As Table 3.1 shows, the relative size of the African American population in southern and border states was declining between 1900 and 1960 at the same time that it was increasing in the Northeast, Midwest, and West. The greatest gains came in large states with an abundance of Electoral College votes. In the 1948 presidential contest, California (25), Illinois (28), Michigan (19), Ohio (25), New York (47), and Pennsylvania (35) accounted for 179 electors. These states were also highly competitive. In the 1948 race, California was decided by 0.44% of the vote, Michigan by 1.6%, Ohio by 0.24%, Illinois by 0.84%, New York by 0.99%, and Pennsylvania by 4%. In the 1960 presidential election, these same six states accounted for 181 electors, and the margins in these states were again razor thin. California was decided by less than 0.55% of the vote,

TABLE 3.1. *The Great Migration: Percent African American population by region and select northern cities, 1900–1960*

	1900	1940	1960	Difference (1960–1900)
Region				
Northeast	1.8	3.8	6.8	5.0
Midwest	1.9	3.5	6.7	4.8
South and Border	32.3	23.8	20.6	−11.7
West	0.7	1.2	3.9	3.2
Select cities				
Chicago	1.8	8.2	22.9	21.1
Detroit	1.4	9.2	28.9	27.5
St. Louis	6.2	13.3	28.6	22.4
Cincinnati	4.4	12.2	21.6	17.2
Cleveland	1.6	9.6	28.6	27.0
Philadelphia	4.8	13.0	26.4	21.6
Los Angeles	2.1	4.2	13.5	11.4

Source: "Historical Census Statistics on Population Totals by Race, 1790 to 1990, and by Hispanic Origin, 1970 to 1990, for Large Cities and Other Urban Places in the United States." Campbell Gibson and Kay Jung. Population Division Working Paper No. 76, US Census Bureau, Washington, DC, 20233, February 2005.

Illinois by 0.19%, Michigan by 2%, Ohio by 6.6%, New York by 5%, and Pennsylvania by 2.2%.

Moreover, the African American migration into northern states was overwhelmingly directed toward urban areas (see Table 3.1). During this period the African American proportion of the population increased dramatically in urban areas, with important political implications. If Democrats wanted to win the presidency, they had to win in states like Illinois, and if they wanted to win in Illinois, they needed to run up big margins of victory in Chicago. African Americans thus became a key component to the Democratic coalition in cities and states throughout the North, particularly as the white vote in both northern suburbs and southern states was becoming more problematic.

The migration of African Americans to the North was typically arduous, and the new arrivals confronted a broad array of discriminatory practices. Unlike in the South, however, African Americans were able to vote, and hence, their presence gave rise to politicians courting their support. This meant that many northern politicians were, for very practical political reasons, being converted to the cause of civil rights.

None of this suggests that northern states presented an equal rights paradise for the new arrivals. Indeed, discriminatory practices were frequently introduced in the northern states as minority populations grew in size and influence. Again, California's Proposition 14 was embraced by white voters in response to the California State Legislature's adoption of the Rumford Fair Housing Act in 1963, forbidding racial discrimination in the sale or rental of housing. Proposition 14 amended the California Constitution before it was declared unconstitutional by the US Supreme Court. (The amendment to the California Constitution was ultimately removed, after the fact, by a vote of the California electorate.) At the same time, it reveals the extent of racial and ethnic tension among whites unwilling to give up property rights as sellers or landlords in the furtherance of racial and ethnic equality.

Progress in civil rights was not simply a matter of changing demography due to population movement, however. American involvement in World War II had been justified as a principled struggle against racially xenophobic totalitarian regimes. The ideology of the American war effort inevitably collided with contradictory impulses – the principled struggle could not be reconciled with resettlement camps for Japanese American citizens or racial segregation within the armed forces or discriminatory treatment of the families of African American and Japanese American soldiers. The war made these contradictions an obvious and pathetic affront both to the democratic principles that justified the war effort and to the sacrifices of American soldiers. This was especially vivid in the context of African American and Japanese American soldiers returning from the war to be treated as second-class citizens.

These issues were central to the political context that set the stage for Harry Truman's desegregation of the armed forces in 1948, as well as his proposed civil rights program in anticipation of the 1948 election campaign. Truman's actions galvanized southern opposition during the campaign. In his inaugural 1948 run for the Senate, Lyndon Johnson campaigned against Truman's program. In his own words, "My feelings are well known in my district and in Washington. And Harry Truman knows I am against him on this program. I just don't think Congress should try to cram his program down the throats of Southern States" (Evans and Novak 1966: 5). Truman and congressional Democrats were marginally complicit in their southern colleagues' opposition, at least in the sense that they gave the latter wide latitude in their actions, political campaigns, and statements opposing the civil rights agenda.

During this same period, union leaders and Democratic Party activists led the way in pushing the party toward a more active party role in the furtherance of civil rights for African Americans (Schickler 2016; Schickler, Pearson, and Feinstein 2010). It is clear in retrospect, if not necessarily at the time, that the ideological momentum of the Democratic Party was steadily pushing in a liberal direction, not only on civil rights but more generally in the area of social welfare.

The hesitancy of many nonsouthern Democrats to embrace civil rights was, as a matter of practical politics, not surprising. The successes of the New Deal partly depended on the cooperation of the southern Democrats. Both southerners and northerners within the party were still hoping to re-create their New Deal successes. Even Hubert Humphrey and Paul Douglas had great respect for many of their southern colleagues (Douglas 1971; Humphrey 1976), particularly when it came to southern populists such as Lister Hill and John Sparkman of Alabama. In contrast, John Kennedy, whose civil rights instincts were not as liberal, was a friend and close colleague of George Smathers of Florida – a Democratic senator from Florida who won office by race-baiting the liberal Democratic incumbent, Claude Pepper (Elliott and D'Orso 1992: 175).

Hence, progress on the civil rights agenda was neither inevitable nor assured. The 1952 and 1956 Democratic presidential candidate, Adlai Stevenson, worked diligently to adopt an accommodating position with respect to the Southern wing of the party. In his 1952 speech in Richmond, Virginia (1953: 153), he argued, for example, that "[a]mong the most valuable heritages of the Old South is its political genius.... A classic example, it seems to me, is the Constitution of the Confederacy." As a consequence, Republicans began to recover lost ground among those African Americans able to vote during the 1950s. The social welfare progress of the Roosevelt years attracted many African Americans to the party, but that progress was reversed in the 1952 and 1956 elections, and Richard Nixon did quite well among African American voters in the 1960 elections.

There were obvious reasons for the continued effectiveness of Republicans at courting African American votes. Not only was the Democratic Party still the vehicle of white supremacy in the South but the 1957 Civil Rights Act also received its strongest support from Republicans. And the biggest source of obstruction continued to come from the southern Democrats, who demonstrated their ability to hold

the Senate hostage with the threat of filibusters on any civil rights legislation they did not support.

Moreover, the 1954 *Brown* v. *Board of Education* school desegregation case had reversed the "separate but equal" doctrine of *Plessy* v.
Ferguson. In doing so, it created the opportunity for the federal government to end legally enforced racial segregation in schools as well
as to energize the enforcement of the Fourteenth Amendment's equal
protection guarantees. In this context, it was the Republican president
Dwight Eisenhower who ultimately (if hesitantly) sent federal troops to
Central High School in Little Rock to end racial segregation in Little
Rock schools.

In short, nine years after the end of World War II, a US Supreme
Court led by a former Republican governor of California (Earl Warren)
endorsed the Fourteenth Amendment's equal protection clause with
respect to race relations, and a Republican president (Dwight Eisenhower)
enforced its ruling. With the benefit of crucial Republican support and
leadership in the House and the Senate, a relatively weak but politically
crucial civil rights bill was adopted. Indeed, a revolution was underway
that would lead to the most dramatic civil rights legislation since the
adoption of the Thirteenth, Fourteenth, and Fifteenth Amendments at
the end of the Civil War. And it was not yet entirely clear which party
would become the champion of the civil rights struggle (Purdum 2014;
Whalen and Whalen 1985).

In the chapters that follow, we treat the period of 1948–1954 as the
beginning of a transition in American politics. Certainly, not all issues
had been addressed, and the struggle between civil rights advocates versus state rights advocates was far from being resolved, but Truman's
actions in 1948 coupled with the *Brown* case in 1954 serve as a turning
point in American political history. In the words of Congressman Elliott,
the *Brown* decision "signaled the beginning of the government's move
toward actually making integration the law of the land" (Elliott and
D'Orso 1992: 133).

The end of this transition occurred during the two-year period of
1964–1965, when the Civil Rights Act (CRA) of 1964 and the Voting
Rights Act (VRA) of 1965 were adopted. At this point, the Democrats
secured their position as the party of civil rights. In spite of crucial
Republican support in passing the CRA of 1964 and the VRA of 1965,
Barry Goldwater's 1964 presidential election campaign inaugurated a
Republican Party more concerned about the preservation of state rights
than about the enforcement of the Fourteenth Amendment. The struggle

over equal rights certainly continues, but the adaptation and evolution of the political parties, as well as the redefinition of the conflict, would be substantially in place after the adoption of the 1964 and 1965 Acts (Carmines and Stimson 1989). Hence, in the analyses that follow, we compare the period from 1940 to 1954 with the reorganized party system in place between 1965 and 1979, as well as consider the political implications for race, class, and social welfare going forward.

4

Civil Rights and Populism

The 1957 Civil Rights Act in the US Senate[*]

The 1957 Civil Rights Act (CRA) was the first significant civil rights legislation adopted by the Congress since the end of Reconstruction. It was passed in the face of seemingly intractable disagreement and very long odds of success. Many otherwise liberal Democrats were still weak on civil rights, while many otherwise conservative Republicans were strong civil rights supporters. Within the political context of the New Deal, the Democratic Party's coalition was held together by two contradictory policy goals: an economically liberal populist instinct combined with the corrupting political imperative of home rule for the white Southern wing of the party. The construction of majority support for the passage of the 1957 Act thus provides a preview of the New Deal Democratic Party's demise, as well as its replacement with a new party system.

The 1957 Act constitutes a watershed moment in the evolution of American politics, even though it failed to produce any dramatic change that would revolutionize the legal landscape of racial discrimination in the United States. The Act served as a turning point in the development of civil rights coalitions in Congress. It revealed the basis of support and opposition to the cause of civil rights, and it proved to be a critical moment in the development and transformation of American political coalitions. In particular, the 1957 Act was the last time that liberal Democrats would fail to be primary supporters of civil rights legislation

---

[*] Professor Jack Reilly is a coauthor of this chapter.

and the last time that the coalition supporting civil rights would be initiated and dominated by Republicans.

Beyond its historical importance, the politics surrounding the Act demonstrates a recurrent tension for liberals in American politics – the historic and continuing difficulty of creating a party that is both populist and supportive of civil rights. Liberal Democrats have frequently found themselves in situations where they have been unable to accomplish both the civil rights goals and the populist goals that have been jointly crucial to the party's success.

CIVIL RIGHTS AND POPULISM: THE CHALLENGES OF MULTIDIMENSIONAL POLITICS

Legislative politics organized along a single dimension can be expected to proceed in an orderly, predictable fashion in which the relative influence of each legislator can be understood relative to the median position regarding a single issue. When a legislature addresses a policy proposal using a majority decision rule, where each legislator's preference can be arrayed from strongly favorable to strongly oppose, the median legislator occupies a position of enhanced influence, with the capacity to cast a deciding vote on whether a bill passes or fails. Even in a context marked by ambiguity and uncertain preferences, voters in the middle of the preference distribution are particularly influential in deciding an issue, while those at the extremes are captives of their own strong preferences.

At the same time, legislators are located closer to the median for a reason, most typically because the issues involved lie beyond the orbit of concerns that mobilize their constituents and thus motivate their own strategy and behavior. Hence, one can say that the legislators who matter the most care the least; they have less at stake with respect to the outcome and are more likely to be indifferent (Huckfeldt et al. 1999). Their own indifference makes them particularly flexible and hence influential in affecting an outcome, as well as in exploiting their strategic advantage to realize their own interests with respect to other independent issues that they view as more important.

While the median voter argument helps us understand the comparative advantages and obstacles facing both those at the median and those at the extremes of a single issue dimension, it provides less guidance regarding the implications of issue spaces with multiple dimensions for the political influence of the various actors. In particular, what are

the implications for policy-making when new issue dimensions are introduced within an issue space?

To explain the passage of the 1957 Act in the Senate, we first charac-
terize the strategic problems that confronted proponents and opponents
of civil rights legislation. We then show how Senate Majority Leader
Lyndon Johnson (D-TX) used the heresthetical manipulation of issue
dimensions to create new networks of interests making it possible to
pass the Act. In contrast to previous research (Jeong, Miller, and Sened
2009), we argue that it could not have been passed without the introduction of a second dimension to legislative consideration.

As long as the legislation involved a single dimension, the Act was
hopelessly threatened by a southern filibuster. Johnson introduced
a second dimension into the debate – public versus private financing
of hydroelectric power in the West, thereby transforming the legislative process and the obstacles that would have kept the Act from being
enacted. The introduction of the second issue dimension enhanced the
relative influence of particular interests – those of southern Democrats
who opposed a strong civil rights bill and a group of populist Democrats
from the Northwest who favored the creation of a public power utility
on the Snake River that borders eastern Oregon, eastern Washington,
and western Idaho.

Just as important, the voting blocs formed during the passage of the
1957 CRA revealed new fault lines with respect to the future of civil
rights politics both within the Congress and within American political
parties. The legislative history of the 1957 Act identifies the new influential actors and issue networks around which civil rights would revolve
during the crucial events of the 1960s, as well as in the recurring debates
in the years that followed.

These legislative networks do not depend on friendship or cordial
relations. To the contrary, our argument recognizes legislative policy
successes and reelection as the primary goals of the professional politician. Successful politicians do not necessarily count adversaries as
enemies or collaborators as friends. Instead, they recognize that important patterns of relations among legislators are built on shared interests.
In this context, two legislators are similarly located within a policy
network to the extent that their interests correspond with respect to
the issues under consideration. Such a model reflects Johnson's own
approach to Senate leadership – coalitions based on networks of shared
interests, as well as a deep knowledge of senators' political (and sometimes personal) strengths and weaknesses.

POLICY NETWORKS AND THE 1957 CIVIL RIGHTS ACT

While the 1957 CRA is often criticized for its limited scope and lack of enforcement powers, it also marked a significant moment in the evolution of civil rights and the reorganization of American party politics. The Act granted African Americans the right to sue their state in federal court for perceived violations of the right to vote, but it was a disappointment for groups favoring more aggressive measures. In particular, the final amended version of the bill contained a provision that defendants (e.g., local voting registrars) were entitled to trial by jury, and the contemporary view was that local election officials could expect a sympathetic hearing from local, mostly white juries. Moreover, the bill only addressed voting rights, ignoring issues related to public accommodations that would be addressed seven years later in the 1964 CRA.

Several factors make the Senate's consideration of the 1957 CRA especially intriguing. First, the deck was firmly stacked against any civil rights legislation, particularly in the Senate. To achieve cloture and end a filibuster, Senate rules at the time required the support of two-thirds of those present and voting. Hence, the opponents could defeat any civil rights bill, and the filibuster had historically stood as an insurmountable obstacle to progress (Katznelson and Mulroy 2012). Second, many nonsouthern Democratic senators were ambivalent over the extension of full civil rights to African Americans. Northern Democrats with (and without) presidential aspirations did not want to alienate southern voters, and Democrats from the West, who had relatively few African American constituents, did not feel an urgency to embrace civil rights. In short, civil rights had not yet become a defining ingredient of the liberal agenda, and many otherwise liberal Democrats took moderate positions on civil rights.

THE STRATEGIC PROBLEMS CONFRONTING
DEMOCRATS AND REPUBLICANS IN 1957

Perhaps the most telling characteristic of the party system in 1957 was the role played by southern leadership in the Democratic Party. Senate Majority Leader Lyndon Johnson and Speaker of the House Sam Rayburn were both Texas Democrats who frequently collaborated with President Eisenhower on many aspects of his political agenda. Many southern Democrats in the House and Senate who, due to their longevity in office, served as influential committee and subcommittee chairs supported them in this effort. Hence, the politics of the 1950s depended on close collaborative relations between a moderate Republican president and the southern Democratic congressional leadership. Moreover, the eleven states of the former confederacy were crucial to the Democratic majorities in both houses of Congress. In 1957, all 22 senators from the 11 former Confederate states were Democrats, and 99 out of the 106 members of these states' House delegations were Democrats as well.

The Republicans, in contrast, realized a significant advantage in Senate seats throughout the rest of the country, with forty-six Republicans and twenty-seven Democrats. Hence, twelve years after the death of Franklin Roosevelt, Democratic control of the Senate continued to depend on the southern Democratic delegation – a group of Democrats who repeatedly showed their willingness to cooperate with a Republican president as well as their willingness to join forces with other groups amenable to accommodating their regionally defined interests – the maintenance of a Jim Crow system of segregation and discriminatory treatment not only at the polling place but also in virtually every aspect of life (Katznelson 2013; Woodward 1938). Regardless of the New Deal revolution, the party system that existed in 1957 looked similar in many ways to the party system that came into being in the aftermath of the Civil War, nearly a century earlier.

A liberal movement within the Democratic Party, composed of both activists and office holders, had been mounting a challenge to the southern hegemony within the party (Schickler 2016). Hubert Humphrey (D-MN) and Paul Douglas (D-IL) led the successful fight to adopt a civil rights plank to the Democratic platform at the 1948 convention,[1] but this success came at a substantial political price. The Dixiecrat candidacy of Strom Thurmond cost Harry Truman the electoral votes of four Deep South states, and Truman was barely able to come away with a victory. In spite of these political headwinds, northern liberal Democrats continued to gain ground in the Senate. In addition, several southern Democratic senators were also cautiously moderating their positions on race – Tennessee senators Estes Kefauver and Al Gore Sr. as well as Texas senators Lyndon Johnson and Ralph Yarborough.

---

[1] At the time of the 1948 Democratic convention, Douglas and Humphrey were (soon-to-be-successful) Democratic Party candidates for the Senate from Illinois and Minnesota, respectively. Humphrey made the dramatic and compelling speech in support of adding a civil rights plank to the 1948 Democratic Party platform.

In short, the cause of civil rights was gaining ground, but with the exceptions of Tennessee and Texas, it was primarily a northern phenomenon in the US Senate.

In contrast, the southern senators were much more heterogeneous on nonracial economic issues (Katznelson 2013; Key 1949). As Katznelson (2013) points out, the South included many poor whites and relatively few corporate interests, and hence, many southern Democrats were strong populist supporters of government programs benefitting disadvantaged whites during the New Deal era. Indeed, they provided an indispensable ingredient to its success. Senators John Sparkman and Lister Hill of Alabama stand as vivid examples of this brand of economically liberal but racially conservative politics. Their Americans for Democratic Action (ADA) scores in the 1956 session placed them in the most liberal quartile of the Senate, at the same time that they were white supremacists and signers of the Southern Manifesto.[2]

Much of the dynamic surrounding the 1957 CRA must also be seen in the context of the run-up to the 1960 presidential elections. Two of the leading candidates for the Democratic nomination were John Kennedy and Lyndon Johnson, and they faced very different political constraints and challenges. As the influential Senate Majority Leader, Lyndon Johnson wanted to lead the Senate to vote for a civil rights act in order to appeal to a wider, nonsouthern Democratic Party. Conversely, John Kennedy provided tempered support for the CRA as part of an effort to make his candidacy plausible to southern Democrats. He voted for the Act's final passage, but he also voted for the controversial Jury Amendment that was seen as weakening the Act's enforcement.

Just as important, Republicans continued to lay their claim as the party of the Great Emancipator, and northern Democrats had not yet fully embraced civil rights for African Americans. Harry Truman's narrow presidential victory in the 1948 election was the first time that the Democratic Party had identified with the cause of civil rights for African Americans, and the fact that he nearly lost the election was not ignored among his fellow Democrats. While many African Americans supported the Democratic Party of Franklin Roosevelt, many others supported the Republicans. Adlai Stevenson made a concerted effort to

---

[2] Hill and Sparkman were certainly not the first economic liberals (or at least populists) who had difficulties reconciling their political instincts on economic issues with the reality of race in southern politics (Katznelson 2013; Woodward 1938).

maintain southern support for his presidential candidacies (Stevenson 1953: 26–28). And Eisenhower received approximately 40 percent of the African American vote in both 1952 and 1956.

Indeed, the strongest support for the 1957 CRA came from the Republicans. They were unanimous in support of the Act on final passage, and the eighteen votes against the Act came almost entirely from southern Democrats.[3] While there was virtually unanimous support outside the southern delegation for the final passage of the Act, a deep partisan divide existed in the rest of the Senate regarding how aggressive the measure should be. A particularly important vote was on the crucial "jury trial amendment" seen among the legislative supporters as the primary vehicle for weakening the Act. Seventy-four percent of Republicans voted against the jury trial amendment, but none of the southern Democrats and only one-third of the northern Democrats voted against it. In short, the Democrats had become the party of the economically disadvantaged but not yet the party of civil rights.

THE JURY AMENDMENT

Under the original legislation crafted by Attorney General Louis Brownlow's Department of Justice, criminal contempt cases would be tried before a judge. The Jury Amendment was central to a series of actions in the Senate that narrowed the scope of the Act, restricting it to issues surrounding the vote as well as making it more difficult to enforce. The vote on the Jury Amendment became crucial to Johnson's strategy of securing civil rights legislation. By creating a toothless lion, he would be able to ensure the cooperation of Senator Richard Russell of Georgia, the dean of the Senate and leader of the Senate's southern Democrats, in allowing the legislative process to move forward. The southern delegation would never support the Act on final passage, but Johnson's goal was to keep them from obstructing the bill's consideration with a filibuster. He needed to pass a bill, but his own

---

[3] The only exception was the idiosyncratic behavior of Wayne Morse, the independently minded senator from Oregon, who was at the time a Democrat. He had been a supporter of strong civil rights legislation, but his support was compromised by the Hells Canyon Dam issue discussed later (Caro 2002). After a contentious falling out with the racially liberal senator Paul Douglas over the CRA and Hells Canyon, he voted against the Jury Amendment aimed at weakening the bill, and then proceeded to vote against the weakened bill at final passage.

presidential ambitions were tied to the South, and he could not afford to pass a bill that would make him a pariah within his own regional base (Caro 2002).

The dilemma facing Senate Democrats reached beyond the presidential candidacy of Lyndon Johnson, however. Beginning with the Great Migration of the 1920s, the northward migration of African Americans accelerated, and underlying political realities began to change. By the 1950s, a Democratic presidential candidate needed the support of African Americans in south Chicago in order to win Illinois' electoral votes, and similar situations were playing out in other northern states as well. At the same time, a successful Democrat needed to maintain electoral support in the Deep South, but the balancing act was becoming increasingly difficult. This is not to say that any of the senators were primarily motivated by the future of the national Democratic Party, but the pursuit of their own ambitions created a larger drama and a defining political moment.

Within this context, the problem that remained for Johnson was to keep his southern colleagues from obstructing Senate action. Russell and others in the southern delegation wanted to support Johnson, but they needed assurance that he could maintain control of the legislative process – that he could deliver on his promise to pass a weak bill. And hence, Johnson needed to secure sufficient nonsouthern votes to block a vote for cloture, and thereby limit the scope of the Act (Caro 2002).

WESTERN POPULISM: HELLS CANYON DAM

A relatively small group of northwestern Democratic senators had been strong advocates for public power in the Pacific Northwest, and the focal point of their effort during this period was directed at the construction of a publicly owned dam at Hells Canyon on the Snake River along the Idaho-Oregon-Washington border. The effort eventually failed, and a string of three smaller, privately held dams were constructed and operated by the Idaho Power Company to take its place. At the time, however, the development of public power was a populist cause, and the northwestern Democrats had allies among other western states' Democratic senators. Their efforts had been frustrated by the powerful opposition of private-sector interests allied with Republican members of the Senate, as well as by indifference among nonwestern Democrats. Hence, they had been unable to pass authorizing legislation for the dam in either the House or the Senate.

Lyndon Johnson perceived an opportunity in their frustration. His strategic vehicle was to foster a log roll between two groups of Democratic senators – the liberal populists from the West and civil rights conservatives from the South. He would secure southern votes in favor of Senate authorization for a Hells Canyon Dam in return for western and northwestern votes that could be used to maintain a conservative version of the civil rights bill. From the standpoint of strong civil rights supporters such as Paul Douglas (D-IL), this was a deal with the devil (see Caro 2002, chapter 38). From Johnson's standpoint of realpolitik, it was a necessary compromise and the key alliance for making it possible to pass the 1957 Act.

Johnson's manipulation of the process – in particular, his introduction of a new political dimension into the bill's consideration – produced a bridge between otherwise divergent interests (Riker 1982). This made it possible to pass the Civil Rights Bill in 1957 over the objections of the southern Democrats but avoided a filibuster that might survive a cloture vote and thus defeat the bill. While Strom Thurmond undertook the longest filibuster in the history of the Senate during final consideration of the measure, his theatrics ultimately failed, absent the unified support of the southern Democratic delegation. It became, in short, a Kabuki drama with no chance of success, played out in the course of the bill's passage.

LIBERALISM ON THE EVE OF THE 1957 CIVIL RIGHTS ACT

To what extent did support for civil rights relate to the economic liberal-conservative divide that existed at the time? We begin by considering legislative voting scores calculated by ADA, the leading liberal advocacy group of the time. The senators' scores were calculated based on a series of votes that the ADA selected and defined as indicating support for the liberal political agenda. Hence, they provide a measure of liberalism, anchored in the context of the time.[4] Table 4.1 regresses the Senate ADA scores on two dummy variables: The first is scored as 1 if the senator was a southern Democrat and 0 otherwise; the other is

---

[4] ADA scores are calculated based on votes taken within a calendar year. Our aim is to observe scores that are not conflated with the events surrounding the vote on the 1957 Act. Hence for continuing members, we look at their 1956 scores, and for new members, we look at their 1958 scores.

TABLE 4.1. *ADA scores for senators serving in the first session of the eighty-fifth Congress (1957) by party and region, with predicted values[a]*

	Coefficient	Standard Error	
A. Least squares regression using regional dummy variables			
Southern Democrats	13.3	6.2	$N = 95$
			$R^2 = 0.40$
Other Democrats	45.1	5.8	SE of estimate = 4.9
Constant	25.6	3.5	
B. Predicted ADA scores for three groups			
Republicans	25.6		
Southern Democrats	38.9		
Other Democrats	70.7		

[a] These scores are based on recorded votes during the second session of the eighty-fourth Congress. For first-term senators, the scores are based on the second session votes of the eighty-fifth Congress.

scored 1 if the senator is a nonsouthern Democrat and 0 otherwise; and Republican senators are treated as the excluded baseline category, and scored 0 on both.

Based on these procedures, the resulting estimated mean ADA scores in 1957 among Republicans, southern Democrats, and nonsouthern Democrats are 26, 39, and 71, respectively. Among the whole chamber, the median score was 41 (and the mean was 45), placing the average southern Democrat very near the median on nonrace issues and hence in a strategically influential position. The influence of the famed conservative coalition can also be seen clearly in Table 4.1. The southern Democrats, as a group, were closer to the Republicans than to their fellow nonsouthern Democrats in terms of the liberalism of their voting records, although a few – particularly Senators Lister Hill and John Sparkman of Alabama – were members in good standing of the party's liberal wing on all issues except race (Brady and Bullock 1980; Manley 1973).

Of the three groups in Table 4.1, nonsouthern Democrats were the farthest from the median. And within this group, the five Democratic senators from Oregon, Idaho, and Washington had accumulated particularly liberal voting records that were distant from the median. They had an average ADA score of 88, placing them in the most liberal bloc of the Senate. Thus, on economic issues, including the federal financing of electric power, the northwestern Democratic senators were among the

TABLE 4.2. *Senate votes on three important measures in the passage of the 1957 Civil Rights Act*

		Nonsouthern Democrats	Republicans	Southern Democrats	Total
Hells	No	7.4%	84.8%	18.2%	47.4%
Canyon	Yes	92.6%	15.2%	81.8%	52.6%
Dam	N =	27	46	22	95
Final	No	3.7%	0.0	81.8%	20.0%
Passage	Yes	96.3%	100.0%	18.2%	80.0%
	N =	27	46	22	95
Jury	No	33.3%	73.9%	0.0	45.3%
Amendment	Yes	66.7%	26.1%	100.0%	54.7%
	N =	27	46	22	95

leading liberals of their time. Public power had become a quintessential populist issue within the panoply of liberal Democratic politics, made prominent by the efforts of President Franklin Roosevelt and Senator George Norris, a politically liberal Republican, in creating the Tennessee Valley Authority.

At the same time, a median voter model based on ADA scores does not go very far in explaining the passage of the 1957 Act. As Table 4.2 shows, some surprising vote patterns appear across the three critical votes – authorizing the Hells Canyon Dam, supporting the 1957 CRA at final passage, and voting against the jury trial amendment. First, in spite of their conservative voting records, the Republicans not only voted overwhelmingly in support of the Act's final passage but they also voted overwhelmingly in opposition to the Jury Amendment that was seen at the time as diluting the impact of the Act. While part of the motivation behind the Republican vote can be seen in terms of partisan support for Eisenhower and a civil rights bill that originated in his administration, it also reflected a definition of conservatism based on economic rather than social and racial issues. In the politics of the time, civil rights opponents such as Alabama senators Lister Hill and John Sparkman were economically liberal populists. In contrast, key supporters of the 1957 CRA, such as Senate Minority Leader Everett Dirksen – perhaps its most crucial Senate supporter – were leading conservatives. Moreover, we see that these conservative instincts prevailed among Republicans with respect to the strategically important Hells Canyon Dam vote, where nearly 85 percent voted in opposition to a public power measure.

While the division of the Republican vote might be seen to coincide with the sincere preferences for economic conservatism and civil rights liberalism, the Democratic vote appears more opportunistic. The non-southern Democrats appear to vote in line with their underlying ideological preferences in supporting the Hells Canyon Dam and the final passage of the CRA, but their votes on the Jury Amendment appear more strategic. Even though they were much more liberal than the Republicans, their Jury Amendment vote was nearly a mirror image of that of the Republicans. While nearly three-fourths of the Republicans opposed the Jury Amendment, only one-third of the nonsouthern Democrats opposed it. Indeed, if we consider the vote on the Jury Amendment absent the southern Democrats, liberalism measured in terms of ADA scores demonstrates a *negative* relationship with support for a vigorous civil rights bill. Everett Dirksen's ADA score was 25, placing him in the most conservative half of the Senate, yet he opposed the Jury Amendment. John Kennedy's ADA score was a 92, placing him in the most liberal 10 percent, yet he voted in favor of the Jury Amendment. Once again, these patterns reflect the deep chasm between the liberal economic populism of the time and the support for civil rights.

This break in the ranks among liberal Democrats with respect to the passage of civil rights legislation in 1957 illustrates two crucial political realities. First, in the political context of the period, it was still possible to be a credible populist and advocate of economic liberalism without being a strong supporter of civil rights. Second, the civil rights movement had not reached the level of influence necessary to command the support of the entire liberal coalition. While elements within the Democratic Party were moving toward a supportive activist role on civil rights (Schickler 2016), many elements of the party were primarily motivated by maintaining the New Deal coalition that depended on the support of white southern Democrats. And at this point in American political history, the survival of the Southern wing of the Democratic Party depended on support for white supremacy and racial apartheid. All this would change in relatively short order as the party coalitions were dramatically reconstructed by race, region, and class.

AN ANALYSIS OF CRITICAL VOTES

Our analysis focuses on three key votes and the resulting division of the Senate into voting blocs: the vote on final passage of the 1957 CRA, the vote on the Jury Amendment, and the vote on Senate authorization of the Hells Canyon Dam. This produced the potential for eight different voting blocs, based on all possible voting combinations across the three bills. Only one senator, Wayne Morse of Oregon, voted in opposition both to the jury trial amendment and to the final passage of the Act. His votes might thus be seen as being inconsistent, supporting a stronger bill but voting against the weaker bill on final passage, and are best understood in the context of his stormy relationship with Paul Douglas during the bill's consideration, as documented by Caro's (2002) masterful legislative history. Hence, our initial analysis eliminates his vote, and we are thus left with six different voting blocs ranging in size from four to twenty-nine senators.[5]

We consider the votes of the senate on these three issues in Figure 4.1. For purposes of graphical presentation, each of the voting blocs is separated into as many as three subgroups, based on the conservative, moderate, or liberal ADA scores of the individual senators within each bloc.[6] For example, both moderates and liberals belong to the bloc that voted "yes" on final passage, "yes" on the Jury Amendment, and "yes" on the Hells Canyon, and thus we divide the voting bloc into two separate ideological subgroups (11 and 12). Each voting bloc is divided into at least two ideological subgroups and as many as three. Each subgroup is represented with a two-digit identification number. The first digit is an identifier based on a shared voting record, and the second digit refers to the ADA-based ideology measure – 1 is conservative, 2 is moderate, and 3 is liberal.

The links in Figure 4.1 represent shared votes. A bold line represents three shared votes. A nonbold line represents two shared votes. For ease of interpretation, a single shared vote is not represented within the graph.

Figure 4.1 shows three clusters of groups. First, at the top of the figure, blocs 3 and 4 are united in their positive votes on final passage and negative votes on the Jury Amendment. They are the racial liberals, and their only point of disagreement is related to the vote on the dam. Second, the two blocs (5 and 6) of southern Democrats at the bottom of

---

[5] Ninety-five senators voted on all these issues. Senator Joseph McCarthy (R-WI) died in office before having an opportunity to vote on any of them. His replacement, William Proxmire (D-WI), took the seat in time to vote on final passage only. By eliminating Proxmire's final vote, as well as the votes of Morse, we are left with ninety-four voting senators who are located in six voting blocs.

[6] The cut points for ADA scores were 18 or less (31%), greater than 18 and less than 58 (42%), and greater than 58 (27%).

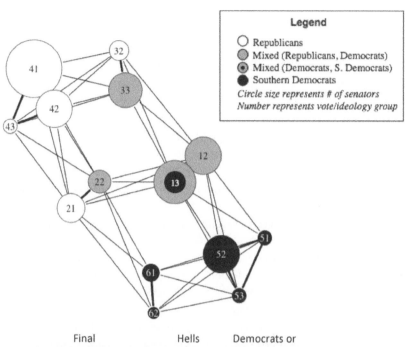

Subgroup	Final Passage	Jury Trial	Hells Canyon	Democrats or Republicans?
12	Y	Y	Y	both
13	Y	Y	Y	Democrats (N.&S.)
21	Y	Y	N	Republicans
22	Y	Y	N	both
32	Y	N	Y	Republicans
33	Y	N	Y	both
41	Y	N	N	Republicans
42	Y	N	N	Republicans
43	Y	N	N	Republicans
51	N	Y	Y	S. Democrats
52	N	Y	Y	S. Democrats
53	N	Y	Y	S. Democrats
61	N	Y	N	S. Democrats
62	N	Y	N	S. Democrats

FIGURE 4.1. Ties based on votes regarding final passage, Jury Amendment, and Hells Canyon Dam. *Note:* The first digit of the subgroup identifies one of six unique voting blocs, and the second identifies the (1) conservative, (2) moderate, and (3) liberal subgroups within the blocs based on ADA scores. The senators in each subgroup can be found in Appendix 4.A.

the figure are united in opposition to final passage and support for the Jury Amendment. They are the racial conservatives whose only point of disagreement is whether they are willing to go along with the log roll regarding the dam. Finally, at the middle of the graph are the two blocs of moderates on civil rights (blocs 1 and 2). These blocs support final passage but vote in favor of the Jury Amendment, and once again they are divided in terms of their support for the dam.

Only three of the voting blocs are homogeneously partisan, and none are ideologically homogeneous. Voting bloc 4 consists of Republicans who take the modal Republican position on all three votes – "yes" on final passage, "no" on the Jury Amendment, and "no" on the dam. The size of a voting bloc represents the number of votes represented in a particular subgroup, and it thus becomes clear that the largest subgroup within the Senate consists of the conservative Republicans who support strong civil rights legislation but reject a public dam. The other homogeneously partisan blocs are 5 and 6, both of which are composed of southern Democrats. One of these blocs participates in the log roll to build the dam, but the other does not. Both groups are conservative on civil rights, voting "no" on final passage and "yes" on the Jury Amendment. Moreover, none of the twenty-seven northern Democrats are located in voting blocs that are homogeneously partisan. They all support final passage of the CRA, but they are divided on their votes both on Hells Canyon and on the jury trial amendment. Hence, neither ideology nor partisanship provides a great deal of leverage in explaining the outcome of the 1957 vote.

Within this context, one liberal subgroup (13) is particularly interesting, composed entirely of both northern and southern Democrats who voted "yes" on final passage, "yes" on Hells Canyon, and "yes" on the jury trial amendment. The voting pattern is easily explained for five of the twelve Democrats in this subgroup – they are liberals who represented Texas, Tennessee, and West Virginia, with state electorates that would have provided little support for aggressive civil rights legislation. Four of the liberal Democrats came from Idaho, Washington, and Montana, and we can assume that they supported the jury trial amendment as part of Lyndon Johnson's log roll. The three northeastern liberals might appear more difficult to explain, except that that they came from states (Massachusetts and Rhode Island) with African American electorates that were neither large nor strategically crucial. Moreover, one of these northeastern liberals (John Kennedy) was preparing to run for the presidency, and southern support would prove crucial to his electoral success. At a strategic level, this bloc is particularly important because it demonstrates the only instance of intersecting votes and ideology between northern and southern Democrats. At the same time, it becomes clear that the voting bloc is held together by temporary expedience.

Figure 4.1 also demonstrates that ideology, as measured by the ADA score, had very little to do with the outcome. All three ideological groups are represented within each of the three major voting blocs. The strongest support for an aggressive bill came from those senators who voted "yes" on final passage and "no" on the Jury Amendment – subgroups 3 and 4, but the largest subset of these two groups consists of the *most conservative Republicans!* Thus, it is important to emphasize that legislators' positions with respect to civil rights were typically independent of their more general ideological orientation. Civil rights moderates were located on both ends of the ideological continuum, from Barry Goldwater with an ADA score of 0 to John Kennedy with a score of 92 and Mike Mansfield with a score of 100. Twelve senators either paired or announced their votes on Hells Canyon: five paired "yes" (3 D, 2 R), five paired "no" (1 D, 4 R), and two announced "no" (2 R). As a group, these senators tended to come from the moderate to conservative wing of the ADA distribution. In constructing Figure 4.1, we use their announced positions in placing them into voting blocs.[7]

The important substantive point is that for much of the Senate at this point in political history, liberal and conservative ideological commitments and voting records had little relevance to civil rights support. Rather, civil rights support was submerged within the boundaries of partisanship and region, and being part of the liberal wing of the Democratic Party was more crucially defined by economic populism.

Hells Canyon can be seen as a classic example of a log roll in which adversaries form an alliance around traded votes, but this particular log roll carried important implications for the evolution of American civil rights policy. The Hells Canyon vote introduced an alternative dimension to the structure of competition, creating an advantage for those blocs located at the extremes of the single dimension defined by positions on the civil rights votes, as well as illustrating the art of political manipulation described by Riker (1982, 1986). Lyndon Johnson and Richard Russell understood that, absent a log roll, the anti-civil rights southern Democrats

---

[7] The likely explanation for not taking a direct vote was either illness (i.e., Matthew Neely [D-WV]) or reluctance to take a formal position. A number of them included conservative Republicans that Johnson needed to be present to avoid a filibuster (Caro 2002: 852).

would lose control of the normal process, and hence would be forced to employ a filibuster. They also recognized, at some level, the need to disrupt the power of the median voter within the Senate on the single dimension of civil rights by increasing the number of relevant dimensions.

A COUNTERFACTUAL EXERCISE
IN ASSESSING HERESTHETICS

Did the introduction of Hells Canyon into the civil rights debate shape the final outcome? To answer this question, we constructed a counterfactual. Four liberal Democratic senators from the Northwest voted for the Jury Amendment: Church (D-ID), Mansfield (D-MT), Magnuson (D-WA), and Jackson (D-WA). None of them was running for the presidency in 1960, and hence we might expect that, absent the log roll, they could have voted against the jury trial amendment. By also including the previously mentioned vote by Morse against the jury trial amendment to the tally, the outcome switches from 52 to 43 in favor to 48 to 47 in favor. In short, a narrow one-vote margin is enlarged to a comfortable nine-vote margin.

Figure 4.2 is based on this counterfactual revision to the historical record, as well as by assuming that Morse's sincere preference was actually in favor of the CRA's final passage. The resulting figure is a simplified rendering of Figure 4.1, absent the Hells Canyon vote, and it allows us to consider an approximately sincere rendering of the underlying support for civil rights legislation. Once again, we see civil rights moderates playing a particularly important role, strategically well placed to determine the outcome of a dispute over civil rights. The problem was that Russell and the southern Democrats would not agree to a moderate solution.

Moreover, the one-vote margin that would have passed the jury trial was too close for southern comfort. Would the liberal holdouts such as John Kennedy have been able to hold out politically if their votes had proved to be pivotal in turning back the Jury Amendment?[8] Russell and

---

[8] In the analysis of actual (as compared to counterfactual) votes, Kennedy was accompanied by eleven other liberal Democrats in voting against the Jury Amendment, seven of whom were northerners. If the four northwestern liberals had voted their likely sincere preferences, only three northern liberal Democrats would have voted the same as Kennedy. Hence, absent the log roll, Kennedy and the other "liberals" might have lacked the political cover needed to vote against the Jury Amendment, thereby putting it in danger of going down to defeat. And Johnson's calculation was that, absent the Jury Amendment, there would have been no bill due to the likelihood of a southern filibuster.

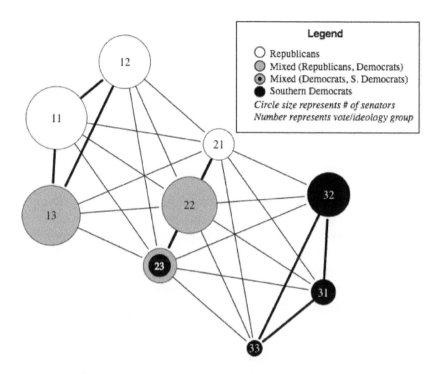

Subgroup	Final Passage	Jury Trial	Democrats or Republicans?
11	Y	N	Republican
12	Y	N	Republican
13	Y	N	both
21	Y	Y	Republican
22	Y	Y	both
23	Y	Y	Democrats (N.&S.)
31	N	Y	Southern Democrat
32	N	Y	Southern Democrat
33	N	Y	Southern Democrat

FIGURE 4.2. Ties based on counterfactual votes regarding final passage and Jury Amendment. *Note:* The first digit of the subgroup identifies one of three unique voting blocs, and the second identifies the (1) conservative, (2) moderate, and (3) liberal subgroups within the blocs based on ADA scores. The senators in each subgroup can be found in Appendix 4.B.

the other southern Democrats were correct to worry about the outcome, and the execution of Lyndon Johnson's strategy solved the problem, if only temporarily. The civil rights moderates occupied an influential role and could have produced an outcome unacceptable to the southern Democrats.

Many of them were the individuals who would turn out to be particularly important as the civil rights agenda progressed. Most ultimately ended up picking sides and determining not only the future of civil rights legislation from 1964 and forward but also the parallel reconfiguration of their respective political parties (Jeong, Miller, and Sened 2009; Rodriguez and Weingast 2003). Returning to Figure 4.2, node 21 includes Barry Goldwater and node 23 includes John Kennedy. In short, these civil rights "moderates" were in fact a very heterogeneous group of individuals with very different ideological inclinations, who were being pulled in very different directions. Senators like Kennedy became civil rights liberals, and senators like Goldwater became civil rights conservatives.

This produced, in turn, a series of transitions among the ranks of the existing civil rights liberals and conservatives. The civil rights conservatives were almost entirely southern Democrats with varied ideological positions in 1957 on issues other than race. As Table 4.3 shows, they were almost entirely replaced by conservative Republicans. The percent Democratic among the twenty-two senators representing the eleven states of the original confederacy declined from 100 percent in 1957 to 14 percent in 2017.

The civil rights liberals – who were an ideologically diverse mix of Republicans and Democrats – would be transformed as well. The biggest change has been that ideological boundaries with respect to race have come into correspondence with the ideological boundaries corresponding to the other primary issue in American politics – economic liberalism. No longer would ADA scores predict economic liberalism but also fail to predict voting records with respect to civil rights. Instead, civil rights became a defining ingredient in the very definition of what it means to be liberal and conservative. This political transformation is a sign of genuine progress in the evolution of American democratic institutions. Largely due to the 1965 Voting Rights Act and its subsequent amendments, African Americans have seized the opportunity to participate successfully in electoral politics. Indeed, as Kousser argues (2008: 667):

[I]ncreasing numbers of African-American officeholders in the Democratic party drove whites to the Republicans, and the white flight increased black influence in Democratic primaries and in Democratic delegations in state legislatures that oversaw redistricting. ... Completing the virtuous circle, as whites became more accustomed to seeing black and brown faces in offices, minority Democratic nominees could often gain enough white support in general elections to beat white Republicans.

TABLE 4.3. *Percent Democratic of the Southern delegation in the US Senate[a]*

Congress	First Year	Number Democratic	Percent Democratic
85th	1957	22	100%
95th	1977	16	73%
105th	1997	7	32%
115th	2017	3	14%

[a] Calculated for the eleven states that formed the confederacy, based on the number of Democrats who held office on the first day of the new Congress.

While the progress is *both* genuine *and* virtuous, it has resulted in a Democratic Party whose presidential candidates have been unable to secure a majority of the white popular votes since 1964. And while the South achieved competitive two-party politics for a time (Aldrich and Griffin 2018), elections in the South have more recently evolved into a color-coded politics placing Democratic candidates at a severe disadvantage. The solid white Democratic South is frequently replaced by the solid white Republican South. As we will see, the statement by Congressman Elliott that began Chapter 3 resonates not only in Alabama but much more broadly throughout the country. Many of the white working-class voters who would be expected to embrace a populist commitment to economic liberalism and social welfare benefits have instead repeatedly chosen to reject social welfare programs that would benefit all races and ethnicities.

CONCLUSION

The politics surrounding the adoption of the 1957 CRA cannot be understood apart from the contradictions and inconsistencies that existed within the core support groups of both political parties in the aftermath of the New Deal. In its wake the New Deal left an incomplete reorganization of American politics, where the great unresolved issue was the role of race in American politics. Hence, in the middle of the twentieth century, each party depended on core constituencies that created serious contradictions in their political appeals.

The Republicans were identified as the conservative party of business and economic expansion while being the party of Lincoln and emancipation. The Democrats were identified as the liberal party of the working class and the disadvantaged, but the Southern wing of the party threatened to nullify this advantage among African American voters. Hence, the "liberal" party included the most conservative senators with respect to civil rights. And the "conservative" party included some of the most liberal senators with respect to civil rights. Indeed, Schickler (2016) shows that liberals in the North were likely to support a more vigorous civil rights agenda, yet the Democrats were internally divided and unable to act in unison.

There was nothing inevitable about the creation of a Republican Party that was the party of civil rights as well as the party of business, industry, and welfare. Neither was it inevitable that the party of the working class and labor unions would be the party of white southerners, and hence a party of racial exclusion. Both parties were constructed within the logic of an idiosyncratic historical experience. This experience created contradictions in the American party system, and these contradictions gave rise to the political obstacles standing in the way of fully incorporating African Americans within the nation's political process.

In the post–World War II period, after millions of African Americans had relocated to urban areas beyond the confines of the South, the stage was set for the New Deal Democratic Party to break apart. Northern Democratic candidates became increasingly dependent on the support of African Americans, as southern Democrats faced increasing challenges to the maintenance of white political control at local, state, and national levels. At the same time, the Republicans were equipped to take advantage of their position as the party of Lincoln and emancipation, but they were not prepared to act as a party of the economically disadvantaged. We see, in the events surrounding the 1957 CRA, a party system that had become politically dysfunctional in very important ways.

The Republican Party maintained its support for civil rights but without any serious effort to incorporate African Americans within the party. As African Americans moved to northern states and cities, the Democratic Party moved toward the mobilization of the African American constituency, and white southern Democrats inevitably made a parallel movement away from the Democratic Party. The transition occurred in stages. Beginning in the late 1940s, whites in the Deep South began to vote for Republican presidential candidates. Then, during the 1970s and beyond, political scientists began to study "dual partisanship" – southerners who identified as Democrats in state and local politics but Republicans in national politics (Hadley 1985). By the 1990s, white southern Republicans had not only been elected to state legislatures as well as to the Congress but they were also ascending to leadership positions within the national Republican Party – Trent Lott (Mississippi) as the Senate Majority Leader, Newt Gingrich (Georgia) as Speaker of the House, Haley Barbour (Mississippi) as chairman of the Republican National Committee, Dick Armey (Texas) as House Majority Leader, and Tom Delay (Texas) as House Majority Leader. The South had become the backbone of the party.

An early and prominent view of partisan realignments (Burnham 1970; Key 1955; Sundquist 1983) is that they are sudden events triggered by critical elections and "precipitated by the emergence of new issues about which the electorate has intense feelings that cut across rather than reinforce the existing bases of support for the political parties" (Carmines and Stimson 1981: 108). In contrast, Carmines and Stimson (1981, 1989) identify the importance of ongoing processes of political change, as electorates are transformed through generational replacement and the evolution of political issues. Hence, they point to the importance of 1964 not as an independent discrete event but as the culmination of a process. In their view, the evolving political context of partisan realignment is both crucial and dynamic, reconfiguring the boundaries for what strategic political actors are able to accomplish (Key 1959).

A careful examination of the 1957 CRA, as well as the larger history of the civil rights movement in American politics, points toward the importance of these changing political contexts, as well as the politicians and political activists who contributed to these transformations (Schickler, Pearson, and Feinstein 2010). Indeed, a never-ending supply of political entrepreneurs acts to impress their own visions and goals on the course of democratic politics (Riker 1986), but their efforts are circumscribed by the evolving political context. Hence, the 1957 Act was an important step in an ongoing process that illustrates a slow but steady evolution that ultimately led to a reshaping of partisan boundaries in both the Congress and the electorate.

The rise of the Republican Party among southern whites has effectively eliminated liberals within the Republican Party and conservatives within the Democratic Party – not just with respect to civil rights issues but also with respect to economic, social, and social-cultural issues. Indeed, we have not just seen the reinforcement of a dominant cleavage but the collapse of almost any other competing cleavage within

the system. Little opportunity exists for populists and economic liberals, such as former Alabama Democratic senators John Sparkman and
Lister Hill to win Senate seats in Alabama, just as little opportunity
exists for a liberal Republican such as former New York senator Jacob
Javits to win a Senate seat from New York. Indeed, the 2017 special
Senate election in Alabama suggests that, as things currently stand, only
a truly reprehensible Republican candidate will fail to win statewide
contests in Alabama. Hence, from this perspective, the era begins to
look like single-dimensional politics with a vengeance – a process that
has yielded two politically homogeneous parties, with strong regional
bases of support generating reduced opportunities for compromise and
accommodation.

The problem is that the driving force behind party support appears
much more closely related to race and ethnicity rather than economic
interests. Once again, no Democratic candidate for the presidency
has received a majority of white votes since Lyndon Johnson in 1964.
According to the *New York Times* exit polling in the 2012 presidential
election, approximately 41 percent of whites, 93 percent of blacks, 71
percent of Hispanics, and 73 percent of Asians voted for Obama. In contrast, 63 percent of those earning less than $30,000 and 46 percent of
those earning more than $100,000 voted for Obama (New York Times,
2012). In short, the spread between extreme income groups was only 17
percent, and Obama came within four points of Romney among higher-
income voters. In contrast, the spread between whites and Asians was
32 percent, between whites and Hispanics was 30 percent, and between
whites and blacks was 52 percent. Hence, one might question whether
the driving force behind these parties is simply or even primarily a
matter of economics or economic self-interest, and whether the party
system sustained by the current constellation of groups can resist the
centrifugal forces of its own inconsistencies. That is, over the long haul,
should we expect that it makes sense for affluent African Americans
to continue voting for economic liberals, or for impoverished southern
whites to continue voting for economic conservatives?

The 2016 election provided no reason to believe that the current partisan divide is either temporary or unstable. Donald Trump's promises
to repeal the Affordable Care Act, as well as his plans to "make America
great again," employed a conservative populist appeal that won a full-
throated endorsement, not only from a large majority of working class
whites but also from much of Main Street and Wall Street. Indeed, the

2016 election was not a break with past fifty years of electoral history but rather an acceleration of the ongoing trends.

While the politics of the 1950s is often viewed as a bucolic period of bipartisan cooperation, the biases of conciliatory politics and the potential for cooperation between the parties came with their own politically debilitating and conflict-inducing consequences both within and between the parties (Schickler 2016). Cooperation between Republicans and southern Democrats, memorialized in terms of the "conservative coalition," served to hold liberal Democrats at bay on issues unrelated to race, while Republican support for civil rights was insufficient to pass aggressive civil rights legislation. With the Democratic Party's embrace of civil rights legislation and the birth of the Republican Party's southern strategy, one party became more consistently liberal and the other more consistently conservative. *And the consequence is a more highly polarized party system in which the Democratic Party has lost majority support among white voters, and the Republican Party has become the home of a regressively conservative white populist rebellion.*

APPENDIX 4.A. *Participants in voting blocs for Figure 4.1*

Bloc/Subgroup	Name	State	Party
12	Bible	Nevada	Democrat
12	Monroney	Oklahoma	Democrat
12	Smith	Maine	Republican
12	Anderson	New Mexico	Democrat
12	Kerr	Oklahoma	Democrat
12	O'Mahoney	Wyoming	Democrat
12	Hayden	Arizona	Democrat
12	Chavez	New Mexico	Democrat
12	Young	North Dakota	Republican
12	Murray	Montana	Democrat
13	Kennedy	Massachusetts	Democrat
13	Kefauver	Tennessee	Southern Democrat
13	Church	Idaho	Democrat
13	Johnson	Texas	Southern Democrat
13	Yarborough	Texas	Southern Democrat
13	Green	Rhode Island	Democrat
13	Neely	West Virginia	Democrat
13	Pastore	Rhode Island	Democrat
13	Magnuson	Washington	Democrat
13	Mansfield	Montana	Democrat
13	Gore	Tennessee	Southern Democrat
13	Jackson	Washington	Democrat
21	Goldwater	Arizona	Republican
21	Curtis	Nebraska	Republican
21	Mundt	South Dakota	Republican
21	Schoeppel	Kansas	Republican
21	Butler	Maryland	Republican
21	Williams	Delaware	Republican
21	Capehart	Indiana	Republican
22	Frear	Delaware	Democrat
22	Lausche	Ohio	Democrat
22	Case	South Dakota	Republican
22	Revercomb	West Virginia	Republican
22	Malone	Nevada	Republican
32	Cooper	Kentucky	Republican
32	Wiley	Wisconsin	Republican
32	Aiken	Vermont	Republican

Bloc/Subgroup	Name	State	Party
32	Thye	Minnesota	Republican
33	Carroll	Colorado	Democrat
33	Hennings	Missouri	Democrat
33	Neuberger	Oregon	Democrat
33	Humphrey	Minnesota	Democrat
33	Douglas	Illinois	Democrat
33	Symington	Missouri	Democrat
33	Langer	North Dakota	Republican
33	McNamara	Michigan	Democrat
33	Clark	Pennsylvania	Democrat
41	Bennett	Utah	Republican
41	Martin	Pennsylvania	Republican
41	Bridges	New Hampshire	Republican
41	Flanders	Vermont	Republican
41	Jenner	Indiana	Republican
41	Hickenlooper	Iowa	Republican
41	Ives	New York	Republican
41	Dworshak	Idaho	Republican
41	Hruska	Nebraska	Republican
41	Cotton	New Hampshire	Republican
41	Knowland	California	Republican
41	Allott	Colorado	Republican
41	Bricker	Ohio	Republican
41	Carlson	Kansas	Republican
41	Watkins	Utah	Republican
41	Martin	Iowa	Republican
41	Barrett	Wyoming	Republican
42	Kuchel	California	Republican
42	Dirksen	Illinois	Republican
42	Payne	Maine	Republican
42	Saltonstall	Massachusetts	Republican
42	Purtell	Connecticut	Republican
42	Smith	New Jersey	Republican
42	Beall	Maryland	Republican
42	Morton	Kentucky	Republican
42	Potter	Michigan	Republican
42	Bush	Connecticut	Republican
43	Case	New Jersey	Republican

(continued)

APPENDIX 4.A *(continued)*

Bloc/Subgroup	Name	State	Party
43	Javits	New York	Republican
51	Russell	Georgia	Southern Democrat
51	McClellan	Arkansas	Southern Democrat
52	Johnston	South Carolina	Southern Democrat
52	Long	Louisiana	Southern Democrat
52	Smathers	Florida	Southern Democrat
52	Fulbright	Arkansas	Southern Democrat
52	Stennis	Mississippi	Southern Democrat
52	Ellender	Louisiana	Southern Democrat
52	Ervin	North Carolina	Southern Democrat
52	Scott	North Carolina	Southern Democrat
52	Talmadge	Georgia	Southern Democrat
52	Eastland	Mississippi	Southern Democrat
53	Sparkman	Alabama	Southern Democrat
53	Hill	Alabama	Southern Democrat
61	Robertson	Virginia	Southern Democrat
61	Thurmond	South Carolina	Southern Democrat
61	Byrd	Virginia	Southern Democrat
62	Holland	Florida	Southern Democrat
Not assigned	Morse	Oregon	Democrat

APPENDIX 4.B. *Participants in voting blocs for Figure 4.2*

Bloc/Subgroup	Name	State	Party
11	Hruska	Nebraska	Republican
11	Hickenlooper	Iowa	Republican
11	Dworshak	Idaho	Republican
11	Jenner	Indiana	Republican
11	Allott	Colorado	Republican
11	Flanders	Vermont	Republican
11	Bridges	New Hampshire	Republican
11	Knowland	California	Republican
11	Martin	Pennsylvania	Republican
11	Ives	New York	Republican

Bloc/Subgroup	Name	State	Party
11	Carlson	Kansas	Republican
11	Cotton	New Hampshire	Republican
11	Barrett	Wyoming	Republican
11	Martin	Iowa	Republican
11	Bennett	Utah	Republican
11	Bricker	Ohio	Republican
11	Watkins	Utah	Republican
12	Aiken	Vermont	Republican
12	Saltonstall	Massachusetts	Republican
12	Bush	Connecticut	Republican
12	Morton	Kentucky	
12	Kuchel	California	Republican
12	Beall	Maryland	Republican
12	Potter	Michigan	Republican
12	Thye	Minnesota	Republican
12	Cooper	Kentucky	Republican
12	Wiley	Wisconsin	Republican
12	Payne	Maine	Republican
12	Dirksen	Illinois	Republican
12	Smith	New Jersey	Republican
12	Purtell	Connecticut	Republican
13	Case	New Jersey	Republican
13	Carroll	Colorado	Democrat
13	McNamara	Michigan	Democrat
13	Humphrey	Minnesota	Democrat
13	Douglas	Illinois	Democrat
13	Magnuson	Washington	Democrat
13	Mansfield	Montana	Democrat
13	Neuberger	Oregon	Democrat
13	Javits	New York	Republican
13	Symington	Missouri	Democrat
13	Clark	Pennsylvania	Democrat
13	Jackson	Washington	Democrat
13	Langer	North Dakota	Republican
13	Church	Idaho	Democrat
13	Morse	Oregon	Democrat
13	Hennings	Missouri	Democrat
21	Schoeppel	Kansas	Republican
21	Williams	Delaware	Republican
21	Mundt	South Dakota	Republican

(continued)

APPENDIX 4.B *(continued)*

Bloc/Subgroup	Name	State	Party
21	Goldwater	Arizona	Republican
21	Curtis	Nebraska	Republican
21	Capehart	Indiana	Republican
21	Butler	Maryland	Republican
22	Anderson	New Mexico	Democrat
22	Frear	Delaware	Democrat
22	Young	North Dakota	Republican
22	Lausche	Ohio	Democrat
22	O'Mahoney	Wyoming	Democrat
22	Murray	Montana	Democrat
22	Revercomb	West Virginia	Republican
22	Hayden	Arizona	Democrat
22	Bible	Nevada	Democrat
22	Chavez	New Mexico	Democrat
22	Case	South Dakota	Republican
22	Monroney	Oklahoma	Democrat
22	Kerr	Oklahoma	Democrat
22	Malone	Nevada	Republican
22	Smith	Maine	Republican
23	Green	Rhode Island	Democrat
23	Johnson	Texas	Southern Democrat
23	Gore	Tennessee	Southern Democrat
23	Yarborough	Texas	Southern Democrat
23	Kefauver	Tennessee	Southern Democrat
23	Neely	West Virginia	Democrat
23	Kennedy	Massachusetts	Democrat
23	Pastore	Rhode Island	Democrat
31	Thurmond	South Carolina	Southern Democrat
31	McClellan	Arkansas	Southern Democrat
31	Russell	Georgia	Southern Democrat
31	Robertson	Virginia	Southern Democrat
31	Byrd	Virginia	Southern Democrat
32	Johnston	South Carolina	Southern Democrat
32	Eastland	Mississippi	Southern Democrat
32	Long	Louisiana	Southern Democrat
32	Talmadge	Georgia	Southern Democrat
32	Stennis	Mississippi	Southern Democrat
32	Holland	Florida	Southern Democrat

Bloc/Subgroup	Name	State	Party
32	Scott	North Carolina	Southern Democrat
32	Ervin	North Carolina	Southern Democrat
32	Fulbright	Arkansas	Southern Democrat
32	Smathers	Florida	Southern Democrat
32	Ellender	Louisiana	Southern Democrat
33	Sparkman	Alabama	Southern Democrat
33	Hill	Alabama	Southern Democrat

5

Race, Class, and the End of the
New Deal in the US Senate*

A number of studies demonstrate a puzzling relationship in American politics. Wealthier states tend to be represented in Congress by liberals typically committed to social welfare spending. In contrast, poor states tend to be represented by economic conservatives typically hostile to greater social welfare spending. The "red state, blue state, rich state, poor-state" phenomenon identified by Gelman et al. (2010) is not due to affluent voters in wealthy states being ardent liberals. To the contrary, the pattern within states is one in which more affluent individuals are less likely to support Democratic candidates than the less affluent. Hence, the pattern arises as a consequence of state-level variations in party support that persist even after taking account of individual affluence.

This red state-poor state relationship is, however, a relatively recent phenomenon. Prior to the 1960s, the relationship had been reversed. The poorest states were represented by some of the most economically liberal members of Congress, and most of these poor states were located in the South. Indeed, at the end of World War II, the American South was not simply the most Democratic region of the country but by some measures the most liberal. It had been crucial to the successes of the New Deal, including the passage of revolutionary labor legislation and the expansion of social welfare programs, and it provided strong support to a war effort aimed at fighting totalitarian threats to democracy. Twenty-five years later, it had become the most conservative region of the country, and Democratic prospects in the region were in sharp decline.

---

* Professor Fan Lu is a coauthor of this chapter.

The successes of the New Deal in passing landmark social welfare legislation – the Social Security Act, the Fair Labor Standards Act, and other measures – depended on the solid support of southern congressional delegations. The problem was that southern cooperation came at an extremely high price – a price paid in the currency of racism, human deprivation, and a betrayal of the US Constitution's Fourteenth Amendment commitment to due process and equal protection of the laws for all Americans. During the years of the New Deal and World War II, the United States in general and the New Deal in particular actively engaged "dubious allies, abroad and at home" (Katznelson 2013: 9).

Twenty years later, the dubious relationship with the racially segregated southern states was in shambles, and the South had become the most conservative region of the country. Moreover, the political implications of the civil rights revolution went far beyond the issues normally considered central to the civil rights agenda. Not only had the advent of civil rights within the liberal agenda created a competitive advantage for southern conservatives opposed to civil rights, but it also led to the adoption of conservative positions on social welfare issues among office holders who had previously been stalwart supporters of the New Deal and social welfare liberalism. Hence, and in contrast to Shafer and Johnston (2009), we argue that the great southern realignment during the decades following the 1950s was motivated by race and not by class (also see Huckfeldt and Kohfeld 1989). Indeed, class is frequently submerged by the rising tide of racially based politics.

The New Deal had created state parties that were relatively homogeneous with respect to social welfare liberalism but heterogeneous with respect to racial liberalism. The civil rights revolution had the unintended consequence of creating American political parties in which both parties were increasingly and consistently homogeneous with respect to *both* civil rights liberalism *and* social welfare liberalism – a polarized outcome that set the stage for rising levels of social, political, and economic inequality across the nation.

CONTINUING PROBLEMS OF RACE, ETHNICITY, AND CLASS

Issues surrounding race have been central to the evolution and organization of American political parties, the ideological bases of the parties, and the class and sectional organization of American party coalitions. Writing in 1949, V. O. Key (p. 5) observed that the "politics of the South revolves around the position of the Negro." What was once viewed as a southern issue unjustly resolved by morally and politically corrupt southern institutions became a national issue when, in the first half of the twentieth century, the migration of African Americans out of the South into northern and western cities led to a set of circumstances that ultimately provided political voice to black aspirations. And this led, in turn, to a dramatic transformation of American political parties.

Racial and ethnic divisions in American society have historically served as a subtext for the organization of American political parties. Issues regarding race have created political boundaries within and between political parties and their office holders that have resulted in a second level of political organization. When the boundaries of the parties are incompatible with this second level of organization, the potential arises for a reorganization of partisan politics.

This chapter addresses the issues of race, social class, and partisanship in the context of the post–World War II transformation of the US Senate. The Senate was a major theater of operations in the struggle for civil rights and racial equality. Members of the Senate, among both Democrats and Republicans, moved to pass landmark civil rights legislation in 1957, 1964, and 1965. These legislative victories constituted a turning point for proponents of civil rights. But the impact of these victories went far beyond the issues normally considered central to the civil rights agenda.

In the analyses that follow, we demonstrate how the incorporation of civil rights into the liberal agenda led to the adoption of increasingly conservative positions on a range of social welfare issues among southern office holders who had previously been strong supporters of social welfare liberalism. As long as policy benefits were targeted at white citizens, the programs were able to secure widespread political support. Indeed, if the choice was either to share social welfare benefits across racial boundaries or to end the benefits, the latter alternative was likely to be embraced.

To what extent was this monumental political change due to the replacement of former office holders by newly elected politicians who reflected the new realities of race and politics in the nation and in individual states? Or were these aggregate changes the result of sitting office holders adapting to the new environment and changing their political stripes? We address these issues below by creating a spatial model that treats social welfare votes separately from other issues. This creates the opportunity to address changing levels of support for social welfare policy by region and party within the Senate, as well as its implications for social welfare support across the boundaries of race, class, and party.

This transformation was not solely, nor even largely, the result of replacement of old senators by new ones. Members of Congress may not alter their true preferences (e.g., Poole 2007), but they do alter their voting behavior based on evolving political constraints related to their own political survival. As a consequence, sitting southern senators in this era adapted quickly to the new political environment in their approach to social welfare legislation. And, an important component of these changes was the dramatic movement in the political preferences of southern voters (Aldrich and Griffin 2018; Elliot and D'Orso 1992; Shafer and Johnston 2009; also Chapter 7).

As long as policy benefits were targeted at white citizens, social programs such as aid to elementary and secondary education were able to win widespread support within the southern delegation. In contrast, if the choice was either to share social welfare benefits across racial boundaries or to end the benefits, the latter alternative was likely to be embraced. Indeed, southern senators' support for social welfare liberalism dramatically declined upon the adoption of civil rights within the liberal agenda. The net result would be the end of the New Deal coalition, as well as the transformation of both the Democratic and Republican parties.

REGIONAL VARIATION IN SENATORS' IDEOLOGY

In this section, we consider the ideological positions held by senators before, during, and after the civil and voting rights revolution. US senators are the highest-visibility national political leaders within the individual states. While an electorate's choice of governor may be based on issues and concerns that are relatively idiosyncratic to the state, the choice of a senator is likely to be a more straightforward ideological and partisan choice related to national politics. Hence, the voting record of a senator is not only an indication of the individual office holder's ideological predisposition but the predisposition of the state's electorate as well.

Within this context, we initially address regional variation in the scores senators received on their voting records from the Americans for Democratic Action (ADA) from 1948 through 2008. These ADA scores are based on the percentage of liberal votes cast by each senator on a set of votes chosen by the ADA, and hence, they vary from 0 to 100 percent. These scores have been analyzed in various ways. Some scholars have used the original scores as they are provided by the ADA, and Groseclose, Levitt, and Snyder (1999) have adjusted the scores to reflect changing means and variances in the definition of ideology. In contrast, Poole and Rosenthal (1984, 1985) employ a scaling methodology to identify underlying ideological dimensions in time – a method we will employ in subsequent analyses.

Our own present purposes here are somewhat different.[1] We are not interested in a definition of ideology that is adjusted for changing perceptions and definitions in time. That is, we are not interested in a time-invariant measure of ideology. Rather, for present purposes, we use the ADA scores as time-specific measures based on the issues confronted in a particular session of the Senate, as these issues are seen in the eyes of the participants at the time. Within this context, our main purpose is to observe the ideological positions of individual senators (and groups of senators) relative to their colleagues. In Figure 5.1 we translate the senators' individual scores into quintiles for each Senate, with LOWESS curves imposed on the scatterplots (Cleveland 1993; StataCorp 2017).[2] Those senators in the fifth quintile are the most liberal, relative to their colleagues, and those in the first quintile are the most conservative. This ideological measure thus provides a senator's position relative to the median position within the chamber, defined relative to the primary issues addressed by the chamber in that session (see, for example, Ho and Quinn 2010).

Figure 5.1 shows the mean ADA quintile for senators from each region organized by time, from 1948 until 2008. The period in question captures the period before, during, and after legislative activity on civil rights. While the civil rights issue was already important in 1948, it had yet to occupy significant space on the congressional agenda. In particular, nonsouthern senators had not been required to take positions on civil rights for African Americans, and it had not become a defining ingredient of liberalism. For example, Senator John Kennedy was seen as a liberal, even though his views and positions on civil rights were ambiguous at best. At this point in time, following the New Deal and in the midst of the Fair Deal, being a liberal had more to do with economic issues and social welfare.

In contrast, civil rights had been incorporated as a central ingredient within the definition of parties and political ideology by 2008. At the same time, many of the defining events in the civil rights movement had receded in importance. This is not to say that liberals or conservatives were of one partisan mind with respect to underlying issues but rather that the civil rights issues were more likely to play out in legal cases and administrative actions. Senate action was still important, but it was also less visible and more likely to deal with issues such as whether

---

[1] For other purposes, in later analyses, we will calculate our own W-nominate scores for social welfare votes, as well as employ W-nominate scores taken from Keith Poole's Voteview website.

[2] In this and all subsequent LOWESS plots, we employ a bandwidth of 0.8.

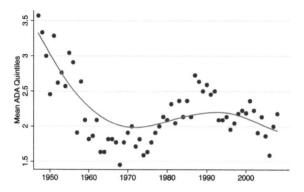

(a) Southern senators' mean ADA quintiles, 1948–2008

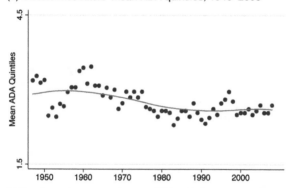

(b) Border state senators' mean ADA quintiles, 1948–2008

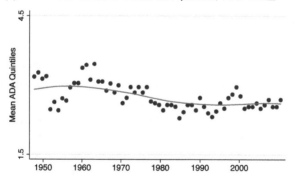

(c) Western senators' mean ADA quintiles, 1948–2008

FIGURE 5.1. Senators' mean ADA quintiles by region, 1948–2008.

(continued)

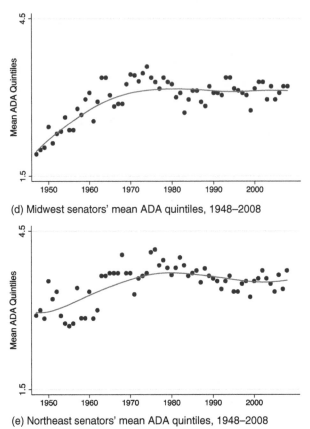

(d) Midwest senators' mean ADA quintiles, 1948–2008

(e) Northeast senators' mean ADA quintiles, 1948–2008

FIGURE 5.1 *(continued)*

preclearance requirements in Section 5 of the Voting Rights Act (VRA) should apply to the whole country or only to areas of the country (almost entirely in the South) with histories of violating citizens' right to vote.[3] These issues were less visible to the public at large and even to the press.

The figure shows very different levels and patterns of change in ideology across the states, and the results are perhaps surprising. In particular, the two highest levels of liberalism at the beginning of the period were in the border states and the South, and the most conservative levels

---

[3] In the 1975 reauthorization, for instance, Sam Nunn proposed an amendment calling for nationwide preclearance. It was defeated by a narrow vote on the Senate floor. Authored by the moderate Democratic senator from Georgia, it was widely seen as a measure to overwhelm the enforcement effort and thereby reduce VRA restrictions on southern states and localities.

were in the Midwest. This reflects the afterglow of the strong support that Roosevelt received from southern and border state senators. It also demonstrates the political dilemma that Roosevelt faced – he could not move forward on civil rights without offending the southern base of his support. Indeed, the backbone of support for the New Deal came from the South (Katznelson 2013), and many (but certainly not all) southern senators were New Deal stalwarts, reflecting the very real problems of poverty faced by whites as well as blacks in the South. At the same time, Roosevelt's vision of American role in international affairs and the wars in Europe and the Pacific had meant increased military spending, and a disproportionate amount of that spending occurred in the South.

The figure also shows precipitous increases and declines in the levels of liberalism within regions. Liberalism declined in an especially dramatic way in the South across this sixty-year period, and the most dramatic declines occurred between 1948 and the mid-1970s, with a short-term resurgence centered on 1990 that quickly disappeared. During this same period, substantial declines appeared in the levels of liberalism among border state senators. In contrast, the most dramatic increase in liberalism occurred in the Midwest. It showed the lowest level of liberalism in the early part of the period, but by the end of the period it demonstrates the second-highest level. Increases in liberalism among northern senators were sufficient to make the Northeast the most liberal region in the country. Indeed, we see something that approaches an inversion of the earlier distribution of liberal strength within the country.

In summary, at the beginning of this period, the core strength of liberalism within the Senate was located in the South and border states, and the core strength of conservatism was located in the Midwest. By the end of this period, the northeastern and midwestern delegations provided the core strength of liberalism, with the core strength of conservatism located within the South. Once again recall that at one point the Speaker of the House (Newt Gingrich), the Senate Majority Leader (Trent Lott), and the chair of the National Republican Party (Haley Barbour) were all southern Republicans. In summary, the New Deal coalition ended with the advent of the civil rights agenda, and this transformation led to a regional realignment among the parties that is reflected in the ideological composition of the Senate.

Of course, we are not the first to connect the regional realignment with the civil rights movement. In their recent book, *Why Parties Matter?*, Aldrich and Griffin (2018, ch. 6) examine the emergence of two-party competition in the South and changes in voting patterns among southern members of Congress. Similar to us, they trace the rise of Republican fortunes in the South to the civil rights legislation of the 1950s and 1960s. Their analysis, however, focuses almost exclusively on broad regional changes, breaking their comparisons into the South versus the non-South. But as this chapter shows, aggregation at the regional level masks a great deal of what happened within the individual states. Indeed, understanding the whole requires a more complete understanding of the parts. In the analysis that follows (and in Chapter 6), we provide more detailed attention to the states of the old confederacy in an effort to map the individual-level changes that were occurring among senators representing the Southern wing of the Democratic Party.

THE POLITICAL TRANSFORMATION OF SOUTHERN STATES

For those accustomed to politics in the late twentieth and early twenty-first centuries, it may be difficult to conceive of the South as a hotbed of American liberalism. By the mid-1960s and early 1970s, southern senators such as John Sparkman and Lister Hill – both from Alabama – were understood as right-wing conservatives opposed to the liberal agenda. They had signed the Southern Manifesto. They supported white supremacy and opposed any extension of civil rights. Sparkman in particular was a military hawk who supported American involvement in Vietnam. Indeed, contemporary definitions of liberalism would exclude the two Alabama senators, or at least treat them as curious contradictions.

During the majority of their careers, however, they were both leading liberals by the definition of the time. Sparkman was a supporter of unions, public housing, education, and public health – certainly issues that continue to resonate among contemporary liberals. Hill was an important backer of the New Deal, supporting government programs on public works, the Tennessee Valley Authority, and public employment, as well as being a central figure in supporting medical research and public health programs. One of the centers at the National Institutes of Health is named in his honor, recognizing his lasting contributions. Both men were central to the successes of New Deal and the Fair Deal legislations.

How should we understand the liberalism of Sparkman and Hill? Both were members of "Big Jim" Folsom's populist wing of the Alabama Democratic Party (Key 1949). Among his many leadership roles in both the House and the Senate, Sparkman chaired the Senate's Committee on Banking, Housing, and Urban Affairs, and he was the vice presidential nominee of the Democratic Party in 1952. Lister Hill was the son of a prominent surgeon and named in honor of Dr. Joseph Lister who had made major advances in anti-septic surgery. Trained as an attorney, Hill served in both the House and the Senate, and he was a coauthor of the Hill-Burton Act – officially known as the Hospital and Health Center Construction Act of 1946. During the early part of their careers, both Hill and Sparkman were consistent supporters of the New Deal and the liberal wing of the Democratic Party, and both developed liberal voting records.[4] Their political paths diverged from the Northern wing of the party in the 1950s, when both signed the Southern Manifesto in 1954, and both voted against the Civil Rights Act (CRA) of 1957.[5]

The decade of the 1950s was a pivot point both in the history of party politics and in the definition of liberalism. When southern politicians realized that they could not be both liberals and white supremacists, they increasingly adopted positions that were conservative across the board. Moreover, this was not simply a process of replacement, where conservative candidates for office were more likely to be elected. Sitting members of the Senate moved their own votes in a decidedly conservative direction. They became even more at variance with the dominant ideological position of the Democratic Party, and thus the Republican Party seized the opportunity to move into the southern political vacuum (Aldrich and Griffin 2018). This meant, however, that the Republican Party had a more difficult time maintaining its traditional role as the party of Lincoln and a champion of civil rights.

In summary, not only liberalism and conservatism but also the political parties in American politics were redefined by the civil rights movement. At the beginning of that movement, the parties were relatively homogeneous on issues of the federal activity in the areas of social welfare legislation and the economy, but they were badly divided on issues related to civil rights. Sixty years later, the parties had become homogeneous *both* on issues of civil rights *and* on issues related to social welfare and the economy. Within this context, the southern populism that led to support for social welfare issues in the 1930s and 1940s has taken on a conservative point of orientation. Hence, the ascendant southern Republicans in the Congress are largely opposed to any increased federal government activity in the areas of economic regulation and social welfare, such as the Affordable Care Act. This has led to several outcomes: a Congress that is more politically polarized and a unified conservative movement that has been empowered by increased levels of support, particularly from the South.

[4] Perhaps the most committed liberal in the Senate during this period, Paul Douglas of Illinois, provides generous retrospective evaluations of Hill and Sparkman, as well as other southern Democratic supporters of the New Deal in his memoirs (Douglas 1971).
[5] Senator Howell Heflin was Sparkman's immediate successor. He was a Democrat with a populist orientation who combined support for a mix of liberal and conservative causes.

REPLACEMENT VERSUS TRANSFORMATION

These patterns of partisan transformation raise an important question. To what extent was the change due to the replacement of former office holders by newly elected senators who better reflected the new realities of race and politics in the nation and in individual states? To what extent were these aggregate changes the result of sitting senators adapting to the new environment and changing their political stripes?

We first address these questions by examining the change in ADA scores for southern Senate seats between 1947 and 1967 – the crucial period in the transformation of the partisan landscape. In 1947, Harry Truman had yet to desegregate the armed forces, and the Democratic Party had yet to add a civil rights plank to its party platform at the 1948 convention. In 1967, by way of contrast, the new position of civil rights within American politics had been redefined. The CRA of 1964 and the VRA of 1965 were in place. The Republican Party had nominated Barry Goldwater, who opposed the CRA. And in 1964 – the first time a southerner was elected president since the Civil War – the Deep South states of Louisiana, Mississippi, Alabama, Georgia, and South Carolina voted for a Republican candidate.[6]

Examining the ordered rankings of representatives has a number of appealing advantages for our purposes. Because the underlying ideological scale in any given session is unobserved, cardinal comparisons between representatives are sensitive to the distribution of proposals brought to the floor (Ho and Quinn 2010). By contrast, percentile rankings are less vulnerable to variation in the distribution of proposals and cut points. As such, finding movement in the relative ordinal rankings of legislators over time provides a strong evidence of change (Ho and Quinn 2010: 846).

Note, however, that changes in a member's ordinal ranking may be due to at least two processes. First, members may shift their ideal points. Second, replacement in the rest of the chamber may alter a member's ordinal ranking. For example, the entry of a large batch of liberal members who replace conservatives will push the rank orders of moderates further to the right, even if moderates did not change their underlying ideal point. The present analyses that follow show that many Southern members moved rightward much faster than member replacement would suggest.

---

[6] The vote of the Deep South was, in another sense, a glimmer of things to come. The 1964 election was the last election in which a majority of white voters supported the Democratic candidate.

Tables 5.1 and 5.2 address ideological change for individual Senate seats, irrespective of the office holder. Table 5.1 displays the original ADA scores, and Table 5.2 displays each senator's percentile rank on the ADA score. In each table the Senate seats are sorted by the original 1947 ADA scores, with the most conservative seat listed first and the most liberal seat listed last.

Tables 5.1 and 5.2 show the high level of ideological heterogeneity of the southern delegation in 1947. The southern delegation was solidly Democratic in 1947, but it was *neither* solidly liberal *nor* solidly conservative (Key 1949). In contrast, by 1967 the ADA scores lie almost uniformly on the conservative end of the scale. Only Al Gore Sr. from Tennessee and Ralph Yarborough from Texas had ADA scores above 50. And only one other southern senator, William Fulbright, had a score above 30.

In short, we can see the individual-level changes in voting records that gave rise to an aggregate redefinition of the South in national politics. Only two of these senators were Republicans – John Tower had been elected as a Republican and Strom Thurmond changed his party affiliation in 1964. At the beginning of the period, the partisan affiliation of the southern delegation was uniformly Democratic and ideologically heterogeneous. At the end of the period, the southern delegation was moving toward partisan heterogeneity, even though it had become increasingly and much more homogeneously conservative.

Tables 5.1 and 5.2 each includes only twenty-one Senate seats because one seat was left vacant in 1947 by the death of Senator Bilbo in Mississippi. Of the twenty-one seats, eight were held by the same office holders throughout the 21-year period. These individuals all demonstrate more conservative voting records at the end of the period, with an average adjustment of –55. In contrast, two of the thirteen replacement senators actually demonstrate a more liberal position at the end of the period, and the average adjustment is –29. In short, we see a remarkable political redefinition of the southern Democratic Senate delegation, led primarily by partisan change among existing southern senators. Not only do they take conservative positions on the expansion of civil rights and voting rights but they also adopt a more conservative position across a range of crucial issues – the issues established by the ADA as the best test of what it means to be liberal versus conservative within a particular session of the Congress.

Table 5.3 employs a series of linear models to estimate the trend in each of the eight senators' voting scores who served for the entirety of the 1947–1969 period. For each senator except Lister Hill of Alabama, a second-order polynomial provides the best estimate of the trend.

TABLE 5.1. *Southern delegation ADA scores by Senate seat, 1947 and 1967, sorted by the 1947 score.[a] Entries are italicized in instances where the same individual served the entire period*

	State	1947		1967		Change
1.	Texas	O'Daniel	0	Tower	8	8
2.	Tennessee	McKellar	10	Gore	54	44
3.	Tennessee	Stewart	20	Baker	15	-5
4.	Virginia[b]	Byrd	20	Byrd	8	-12
5.	Louisiana	Overton	30	Long	15	-15
6.	North Carolina	Hoey	40	Ervin	15	-25
7.	Louisiana	*Ellender*	50	Ellender	23	-27
8.	Virginia	Robertson	50	Spong	23	-27
9.	Arkansas	*McClellan*	60	McClellan	15	-45
10.	Georgia	George	60	Talmadge	8	-52
11.	Florida	*Holland*	60	Holland	15	-45
12.	Texas	Connally	70	Yarborough	62	-8
13.	South Carolina	Maybank	70	Thurmond	0	-70
14.	Georgia	*Russell*	70	Russell	8	-62
15.	Mississippi	*Eastland*	70	Eastland	8	-62
16.	North Carolina	Umstead	70	Jordan	8	-62
17.	Arkansas	*Fulbright*	80	Fulbright	38	-42
18.	Alabama	*Hill*	90	Hill	15	-75
19.	Alabama	*Sparkman*	90	Sparkman	8	-82
20.	South Carolina	Johnston	90	Hollings	8	-82
21.	Florida	Pepper	90	Smathers	23	-67

[a] Mississippi's Theodore Bilbo died during his term of office in 1947 and was not rated by the ADA. His successor, John Stennis, had ADA scores of 44 in 1948 and 0 in 1967, for a change of -44.
[b] Harry Byrd Jr. succeeded his father – Harry Byrd Sr. – in 1965.

TABLE 5.2. *Southern delegation ADA percentile scores by Senate seat, 1947 and 1967, sorted by the 1947 score.*[a] *Entries are italicized in instances where the same individual served the entire period. Higher scores denote a more liberal percentile*

	State	1947		1967		Change
1.	Texas	O'Daniel	1	Tower	18	17
2.	Tennessee	McKellar	19	Gore	61	42
3.	Tennessee	Stewart	31	Baker	26	-5
4.	Virginia[b]	*Byrd*	31	*Byrd*	18	-13
5.	Louisiana	Overton	41	Long	26	-15
6.	North Carolina	Hoey	50	Ervin	26	-24
7.	Louisiana	*Ellender*	57	*Ellender*	36	-21
8.	Virginia	Robertson	57	Spong	36	-21
9.	Arkansas	*McClellan*	65	*McClellan*	26	-39
10.	Georgia	George	65	Talmadge	18	-47
11.	Florida	*Holland*	65	*Holland*	26	-39
12.	Texas	Connally	73	Yarborough	68	-5
13.	South Carolina	Maybank	73	Thurmond	1	-72
14.	Georgia	*Russell*	73	*Russell*	18	-54
15.	Mississippi	*Eastland*	73	*Eastland*	18	-65
16.	North Carolina	Umstead	73	Jordan	18	-65
17.	Arkansas	*Fulbright*	82	*Fulbright*	48	-34
18.	Alabama	Hill	91	Hill	26	-65
19.	Alabama	*Sparkman*	91	*Sparkman*	18	-73
20.	South Carolina	Johnston	91	Hollings	18	-73
21.	Florida	Pepper	91	Smathers	36	-55

Average change = −34.6

[a] Mississippi's Theodore Bilbo died during his term of office in 1947 and was not rated by the ADA. His successor, John Stennis, had original ADA scores of 44 in 1948 and 0 in 1967.

[b] Harry Byrd Jr. succeeded his father – Harry Byrd Sr. – in 1965.

TABLE 5.3. *Estimated trends in ADA scores among southern senators serving at least twenty years beyond 1947, absent civil rights votes (standard errors in parentheses)*

	Time	Time^2	Constant	N = Years	R^2	Standard Error of Estimate
Fulbright of Arkansas	-2.22 (1.66)	0.07 (0.06)	63.3 (9.7)	28	0.08	18.35
	-0.36 (0.43)		55.2 (6.8)	28	0.03	18.47
Sparkman of Alabama	-6.41 (1.27)	0.12 (0.04)	103.4 (8.5)	32	0.72	17.00
	-2.65 (0.37)		84.6 (6.6)	32	0.63	19.25
Russell of Georgia	-4.54 (1.34)	0.12 (0.06)	50.0 (6.8)	23	0.60	11.80
	-1.80 (0.38)		40.0 (5.2)	23	0.51	12.73
McClellan of Arkansas	-2.80 (0.88)	0.07 (0.03)	36.1 (5.7)	31	0.40	11.32
	-.82 (0.24)		26.6 (6.2)	31	0.28	12.14
Eastland of Mississippi	-3.80 (0.83)	0.09 (0.03)	39.3 (5.6)	32	0.51	11.202
	-0.88 (0.25)		24.8 (4.6)	32	0.29	13.26
Ellender of Louisiana	-3.51 (1.42)	0.10 (0.06)	48.7 (7.0)	24	0.41	12.46
	-1.28 (0.38)		40.6 (5.1)	24	0.34	12.92
Hill of Alabama	-.14 (1.90)	0.18 (0.09)	85.2 (8.6)	22	0.79	14.69
	-4.01 (0.53)		98.2 (6.6)	22	0.74	15.91
Holland of Florida	-3.88 (1.53)	0.09 (0.06)	51.5 (7.6)	24	0.51	13.48
	-1.79 (0.41)		43.8 (5.4)	24	0.47	13.78

As Figure 5.2 shows, the common pattern is a precipitous decline in the ADA scores at the beginning of the period, followed by a slower rate of change at the end of the period. Hill provides the exception, with a steady rate of decline in liberal voting over the entire 21-year period. In short, we see a vivid demonstration of southern Democratic senators running for cover. They are not simply voting against civil rights measures; they are also distancing themselves from the entire liberal social welfare agenda.

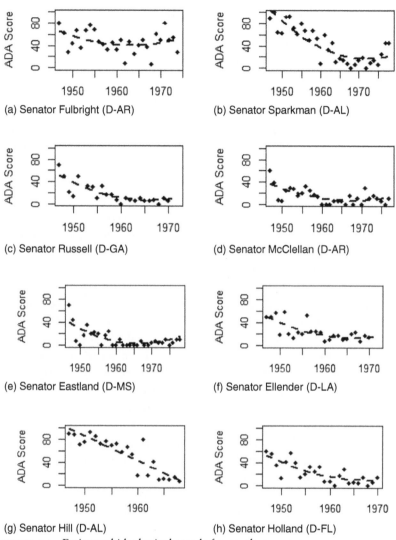

FIGURE 5.2. Estimated ideological trends for southern senators.

THE TRANSFORMATION OF THE LIBERAL COALITION

The transformation of American political parties was not, however, solely an issue of the southern Democrats becoming more conservative. It also involved every region of the country and both the Democratic and Republican parties. We proceed by addressing two tasks. First, we take advantage of the dynamic nature of roll-call votes to undertake analyses based both on independent cross sections and on panel analyses of senators and senate seats across time. Second, we address a problem in the calculation of the ADA scores, given our purposes. The ADA scores are based on votes taken in the House and the Senate on issues defined as important to the liberal agenda by the ADA at that particular point in time. A small proportion of these votes are civil rights related, and hence, for our purposes we removed civil rights votes and recalculated ADA scores without civil rights votes. This provides a measure that more closely approximates support for social welfare measures, absent civil rights.

Table 5.4 treats ADA scores based on roll-call votes for the Senate in 1947 and 1968 as independent cross sections. The unit of analysis is thus an individual Senate seat, regardless of who holds the office. In addition, the ADA score is translated into a rank-ordered score for each Senate seat, both in 1947 and in 1968. Thus, each senator receives a score based on his or her ranking on the score in the Senate, where the more liberal scores have higher rankings. (Recall that civil rights votes were removed in a recalculation of the ADA scores.)

In Part A of Table 5.4, we consider the South defined in terms of the states of the confederacy, relative to the rest of the country. Hence, we employ two dummy variables – one for southern states versus nonsouthern and one for 1968 versus 1947. Based on the coefficients obtained in Part A, the mean rank of southerners in 1947 was 18 points *higher* than the mean rank of nonsoutherners. In contrast, the mean rank of southern senators in 1968 was 29 points *lower* than the mean rank of nonsoutherners. And the *t*-value for the difference-in-differences estimator is 5.26.[7] In short, we see a radical reorganization of the Senate with respect to liberalism defined apart from civil rights.

---

[7] Difference-in-differences estimators measure the change across two time periods either for independent pooled cross sections or for panel data, and hence are particularly useful in the context of measuring changes in legislative vote scores. See Wooldridge (2009) and Wooldridge (2002).

TABLE 5.4. *Rank ordering of Senate seats based on adjusted ADA scores for semi-independent cross sections in 1947 and 1968 by region and year*

A. South versus non-South

	Coefficient	Standard Error	t	
South	17.84	6.33	2.82	$N = 190$
Y68	11.59	4.23	2.75	$R^2 = 0.14$
South × Y68	−46.65	8.87	−5.26	Root MSE = 25.6
Constant	43.51	2.99	14.54	

Predicted rank orderings for southern and nonsouthern states

	1947	1968
South	62	27
Non-South	44	56

B. All regions with north as baseline, controlling for party

	Coefficient	Standard Error	t	
South	−13.56	7.76	1.75	$N = 190$
West	−1.45	6.55	0.22	
Border	−5.91	0.83	0.67	$R^2 = 0.47$
Midwest	−2.70	6.36	0.42	
Y68	30.05	6.93	4.33	Root MSE = 20.4
South × Y68	−40.76	10.18	4.00	
West × Y68	−27.90	9.11	3.06	
Border × Y68	−14.00	12.36	1.13	
Midwest × Y68	−20.90	8.89	2.35	
Democrat	43.03	5.89	7.31	
Democrat × Y68	−21.40	7.43	2.88	
Constant	31.89	4.81	6.64	

Predicted rank orderings for Democratic senators by region

	1947	1968
Southern Democrats	61	29
Northern Democrats	75	84
Midwest Democrats	72	60
Border state Democrats	69	64
Western Democrats	74	55

Y68 = 1 if year is 1968, 0 otherwise.
South = 1 if southern state; 0 otherwise.
West = 1 if western state; 0 otherwise.
Border = 1 if border state; 0 otherwise.
Midwest = 1 if Midwest state; 0 otherwise.
Democrat = 1 if senator is a Democrat; 0 otherwise.

We repeat this analysis in Part B of Table 5.4, not only for the South versus the non-South but rather for the South versus the western, border, and midwestern states relative to the northern states as a baseline. And in this instance, we include controls for party. The difference-in-differences estimator for the South is still pronounced: The mean ranking of the South drops by 32 points from 1947 to 1968. Indeed, the mean rank of Democratic senators in every region except the North becomes more conservative during this period, while the mean rank of northern senators increases by 9 points.

Notice also that the mean rank of Democrats relative to Republicans was higher in 1947 than in 1968. How can this be? Remember that we are taking into account the dramatic decline of liberal rankings among the southern delegation, which in this time interval was still almost entirely Democratic. As time passed, many of the southern Democrats began to look like Republicans, and indeed, many would ultimately be replaced by Republicans.

In short, these rankings demonstrate a profound decline in mean liberalism among southern senators, as well as an increase in mean liberalism among northern senators. These rankings are independent of the senators' civil rights votes, and hence, it becomes clear that the reorganization of political coalitions during the 1950s and 1960s redefined the basis of liberalism and dramatically altered the basis of support for the liberal agenda.

WHAT MAKES THE SOUTH DIFFERENT?

While Key (1949: 5) argued that the politics of race was the central factor in explaining the politics of the South, we are not suggesting that contemporary American politics can be seen that simply. We are, however, arguing that racial politics and the legacy of racial politics go a long way in defining the context of our current political institutions and processes. The politics of race and ethnicity have become much more complex in the intervening seventy years. Not only race but national origin and immigration status also loom particularly large as competing bases of racial-ethnic divides that are often realized both nationally and locally.

The characteristic of race that made it particularly important in the South, and hence made the South particularly different, was the relative size of the African American population. In 1940, 49 percent of Mississippi's population was African American, as well as 43 percent of South Carolina's, 36 percent of Louisiana's, and 35 percent of Alabama's.

TABLE 5.5. *Change in rank order of individual Senate seats based on adjusted ADA ratings, by changing level of racial voting in the nation, weighted by the proportion of African Americans in the state, and by changes in the partisanship of the Senate seat*

	Coefficient	Standard Error	t	Coefficient	Standard Error	t
Weighted racial voting	-3.74	1.15	-3.25	-2.58	1.06	2.44
Partisan change				33.11	6.71	4.94
Constant	4.27	6.08	2.34	6.13	5.76	1.06
N		92			91	
R^2		0.10			0.29	
Root MSE		39.8			35.5	

Weighted racial voting: Percent Democratic of presidential voters among blacks minus the percent Democratic of presidential voters among whites in 1948 and 1968, weighted by the proportion of the state's population that is African American in 1940 and 1970.

Partisan change in Senate seat: 0 = same party controlled the seat in 1947 and 1968; -1 = the Democrats lost the seat; 1 = the Democrats gained the seat.

In Key's words (1949: 5), "The hardcore of the political South... is made up of those counties and sections of the southern states in which Negroes constitute a substantial proportion of the population." In these cases, and at this time, a major political preoccupation revolved around the maintenance of control by white voters.

In Table 5.5 we employ a panel design to examine the behavior of senators over time, not as a function of region but rather as a function of the African American percentage of the population, weighted by the national mobilization of African Americans in support of the Democratic Party. So long as African Americans were unable to participate meaningfully in politics, their numerical threat to white dominance in the South was kept under control. This began to change in the 1940s and 1950s, however, as many northern Democrats began to champion civil rights and civil liberties for all citizens, regardless of race. As a consequence, support for the Democratic Party began to increase among African Americans when they were able to vote.

Hence, we employ a state-level variable that is the percentage of state inhabitants who are African American weighted by the level of racial voting across the nation. This latter index of racial voting (12 for 1948 and 56 for 1968) is taken from Abramson, Aldrich, and Rohde (2012) and defined as the national percentage of African Americans who voted Democratic in the presidential election minus the national proportion of whites who voted Democratic. Thus, rather than simply defining the states by region, we employ a state-level measure that considers the changing national political landscape within the context of the state's racial composition.

We estimate the model using the following difference-in-differences design:

$$y_{it} = b_0 + \delta_0 T + \beta_1 x_{it} + a_i + u_{it}$$

where
y_{it} = the ideological rank of the ith senator at time t
$T = 0$ for 1947 and 1 for 1968
x_{it} = the state's racial political context for ith senator at time t
a_i = time constant unobserved factors affecting y_{it}
u_{it} = idiosyncratic error

Hence,

$$y_{i68} - y_{i47} = \delta_0 + \beta_1(x_{i68} - x_{i47}) + u_{i68} - u_{i47}$$

or

$$\Delta y_i = \delta_0 + \beta_1 \Delta x_i + \Delta u_i$$

The model is estimated in Table 5.5, with and without a partisan change measure for the current senator holding the seat. As the estimates show, we see a decline in the rank order of the Senate seat's ADA score as a function of the racial political context of the state, *regardless* of the control for partisan change in the Senate seat. Estimates in the first column show that, across the range of weighted racial voting (0–14.7), the rank of a Senate seat is predicted to decline by fifty-five positions.

Adding the partisan change variable slightly reduces the racial voting coefficient, but it remains negative and discernible. In this column, the rank is predicted to decline by thirty-eight rank order positions across the range of the weighted racial voting index.

Figure 5.3 shows the scatterplot of the change in a Senate seat's rank order on the change in racial voting. All seats in the lower right area of the plot, with a change of nine or greater rank order positions, are southern states. In short, and as Key (1949) suggested, the role of African Americans in southern politics, and hence in the nation, continued to be pivotal.

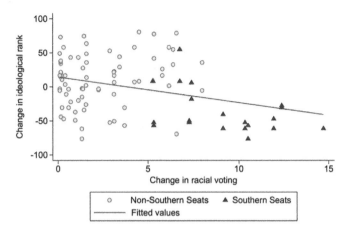

FIGURE 5.3. Ideological rank of a Senate seat by change in racial voting, 1947–1968.

SUPPORT FOR SOCIAL WELFARE

The previous sections showed the dramatic regional and individual changes in the location of support for liberal policies, as measured by ADA scores. While ADA scores represent one metric of support for social welfare, they also include a number of other issues related to definitions of liberalism – such as foreign policy, environmental policy, firearm regulation, and so on. Hence, in this section we consider an explicit measure of support for social welfare policy over the same time period. To this end, we construct a measure based on Aage Clausen's (1973) historical identification of votes in the Congress on social welfare and updated by Voteview (Lewis et al. 2020). We scale these votes with W-nominate scaling procedures. As discussed earlier, because the cardinal values of W-nominate scores are not comparable over time, we rank-ordered representatives in each year and then converted these rank orderings into percentile rankings. The most liberal members in a session are at the 1st percentile, the median is at the 50th percentile, and the most conservative at the 100th percentile.

We begin by examining the broad regional and partisan change in the Senate between 1946 and 1976. Figure 5.4 displays the regional variation of Senate member percentile rankings on our social welfare scores across this period. During the pre–civil rights period, southern Democrats ranked toward the liberal end of the spectrum. While not as liberal as northern Democrats, the southerners nevertheless were much closer to

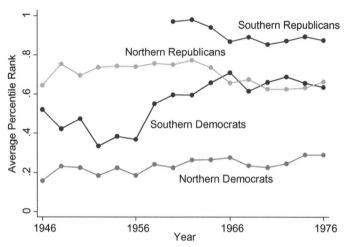

FIGURE 5.4. Regional and party shifts in social welfare percentile rankings, 1946–1976.

northern Democrats than to Republicans. During the era of civil rights legislation (1957–1967), the South shifted abruptly in a conservative direction. By the end of the period, southern Democrats had become among the more conservative bloc of senators, closely resembling Republicans.

The change within the South precedes the full-blown partisan replacement of Democrats by Republicans. To be sure, the southern Republicans who entered were among the most conservative on social welfare. But during this period their numbers were few. In the ninetieth Congress (1967–1968), 86 percent of southern senators were Democrats (nineteen out of twenty-two). The bulk of the southern transformation occurred among Democrats. In short, this figure suggests that the changes were not simply due to changes in the partisan divisions within the Senate but more fundamentally due to ideological changes that were occurring within Senate party memberships (Hood, Kidd, and Morris 1999; Shafer and Johnston 2009). In short, a fundamental ideological redefinition of the parties on social welfare took place.

To what extent was change toward social welfare due to the replacement of former office holders by newly elected senators who better reflected the new realities of race and politics in the nation and in individual states? Or were these aggregate changes the result of sitting senators adapting to the new environment and changing their political stripes?

As in the previous sections, we address these questions by considering the change in social welfare rankings for southern Senate seats

TABLE 5.6. *Southern delegation percentile rankings on social welfare votes (based on W-nominate scaling) by Senate seat, 1947 and 1967, sorted by the 1947 percentile ranking. Entries are italicized in instances where the same individual served the entire period. Lower scores denote a more liberal ranking*

State	Name	1947–1948	Senator	1967–1968	Change
Adaptation					
Alabama	*Hill*	*18*	*Hill*	*68*	*50*
Alabama	*Sparkman*	*21*	*Sparkman*	*63*	*42*
Louisiana	*Ellender*	*30*	*Ellender*	*70*	*40*
Arkansas	*Fulbright*	*36*	*Fulbright*	*47*	*11*
Georgia	*Russell*	*37*	*Russell*	*97*	*60*
Florida	*Holland*	*47*	*Holland*	*93*	*46*
Mississippi	*Stennis*	*63*	*Stennis*	*96*	*33*
Arkansas	*McClellan*	*78*	*McClellan*	*84*	*8*
Mississippi	*Eastland*	*79*	*Eastland*	*99*	*20*
Mean		45		80	35
Replacement					
Florida	Pepper	3	Smathers	65	62
South Carolina	Johnston	20	Hollings	71	51
Texas	Connally	27	Yarborough	07	−20
South Carolina	Maybank	32	Thurmond	99	67
North Carolina	Umstead	45	Jordan	81	36
North Carolina	Hoey	56	Ervin	86	30
Georgia	George	67	Talmadge	75	8
Tennessee	McKellar	69	Gore	40	−29
Tennessee	Stewart	72	Baker	67	−5
Louisiana	Overton	75	Long	60	−15
Virginia	Robertson	82	Spong	61	−21
Virginia	H Byrd, Sr.	93	H Byrd, Jr.	85	−8
Texas	O'Daniel	97	Tower	94	−3
Mean		57		69	12

between 1947 and 1967 – the crucial period in the transformation of the partisan landscape. As we have seen, the most dramatic change occurred in the South, and Table 5.6 addresses ideological change for individual Senate seats, irrespective of the office holder. The Senate seats are sorted by the 1947 social welfare ranking, with the most liberal seats listed first and the most conservative seats listed last. The table shows the ideological heterogeneity of the southern delegation in 1947. The southern delegation was solidly Democratic in 1947, but it was *neither* solidly liberal *nor* solidly conservative on social welfare (Key 1949). In contrast, by 1967 the social welfare scores lie almost uniformly on the conservative end of the scale. Only Al Gore Sr. from Tennessee, Ralph Yarborough from Texas, and William Fulbright from Arkansas had a score below 0.5.

Even before the Republican revolution in the South, one can see the individual-level changes in voting records that gave rise to the aggregate redefinition of the South in national politics. Only two of these senators were Republicans – John Tower had been elected as a Republican and Strom Thurmond changed his party affiliation to Republican in 1964. At the beginning of the period, the partisan affiliation of the southern delegation was uniformly Democratic and ideologically heterogeneous (Black and Black 2002). At the end of the period, the southern delegation was moving toward partisan heterogeneity, even though it had already become increasingly and more homogeneously conservative.

While the southern Senate delegation became more conservative overall, much of the change in the ideological makeup of the Senate was due to changing voting records among sitting senators. All the senators who were in office throughout the period moved in a more conservative direction, and the changes were often dramatic. Sparkman's percentile ranking increased by 42 points, Hill's by 50, Russell's by 60, Fulbright's by 11, Holland's by 46, McClelland's by 8, Eastland by 20, Stennis by 33, and Ellender's by 40.

The Democratic members of the southern congressional delegation who had been notable for their strongly populist inclinations, as well as for their strong support of liberal New Deal programs, went into full retreat. They changed their positions on the ideological issues of the day. The decline in support for the social welfare agenda is particularly striking among continuing senators who had been committed New Dealers: Sparkman and Hill of Alabama, Ellender of Louisiana, Holland of Florida, and Russell of Georgia. In short, if social welfare legislation was to be race neutral, southern Democrats were exiting the social welfare coalition, even though in numerous instances that meant a declining commitment to the provision of social welfare benefits to their constituents. While many of these Democrats were ultimately replaced by Republicans (Black and Black 2002), the first stage in the political realignment came not simply in terms of opposition to civil rights but also in terms of southern Democrats who deserted the party's liberal and social welfare agendas.

SOCIAL WELFARE AND CIVIL RIGHTS OVER TIME

The previous sections examined individual-level changes in social welfare voting. This section analyzes aggregate voting patterns on the issues of social welfare and civil rights in Congress. The analysis relies on the cutting angles of roll-call voting produced by Poole and Rosenthal's scaling procedure (1985, 1997). First, we need to explain what a cutting angle is and what it means. The cutting line is the estimated line that best separates the "yea" from "nay" votes on an individual roll call. Those on one side of the cutting line are predicted to vote in one direction, and those on the other side of the cutting line are in opposition. The angle of the cutting line, in two-dimensional space, can then be used to infer whether a particular roll call divides members along the traditional first dimension of economic liberal-conservatism, or whether the roll call divides members based on some other consideration – such as partisanship or race (Noel 2016; Poole and Rosenthal 1997).

As an illustration, Figure 5.5 presents an example using the DW-nominate scores from 1947 to 1948. The x-axis is the first dimension of the DW-nominate scale. The y-axis is the second dimension of the DW-nominate scale. Panel A of Figure 5.5 shows a hypothetical cutting line angle that is *less than 90 degrees*. In this context, this is a roll-call vote that divides the chamber along party lines. In 1947–1948 a vote like this would have southern Democrats (labeled "SD") voting with northern Democrats (labeled "ND") in opposition to Republicans.

One can therefore treat an angle less than 90 degrees as akin to a party-line vote (Noel 2016). At the same time, this kind of vote does not perfectly map onto the traditional liberal-versus-conservative economic divide of the first dimension. In this example, the economically moderate Democrats, many of them southern, are voting with economically liberal Democrats, many of them northern. Likewise, economically moderate Republicans are voting with economically conservative Republicans.

In Panel B, the angle of the cutting line is greater than 90 degrees. This is a vote that cuts across party lines. In the hypothetical example (again using DW-nominate scores from 1947 to 1948), southern Democrats are voting together with a bloc of Republicans. Likewise a bloc of Republicans are voting with northern Democrats. An issue like civil rights in the mid-twentieth century would be a classic example. Thus, an angle greater than 90 degrees is akin to a vote that divides the parties and where the second dimension comes into play in predicting the outcome.

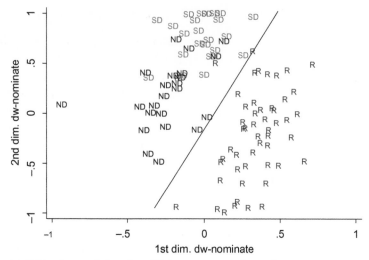

(a) Cutting line angle less than 90 degrees – party line voting

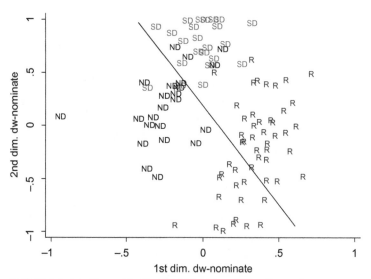

(b) Cutting line angle greater than 90 degrees – splitting the parties, second-dimension issues

FIGURE 5.5. Examples of roll-call cutting line angles.

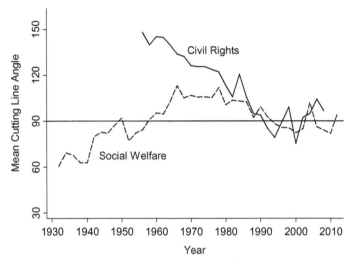

FIGURE 5.6. Mean cutting line angles on social welfare and civil rights roll-call votes, 1932–2012.

Turning to the overtime patterns, Figure 5.6 shows the average cutting line angle in each Congress, from 1932 to 2012, on roll-call votes categorized as dealing with social welfare (Clausen 1973; Voteview [https://voteview.com]). The social welfare category includes issues such as federal aid for education, housing, labor relations, public health, Social Security, and Medicaid. For the period from 1932 through the 1950s, the cutting line angles are generally less than 90 degrees. This indicates that social welfare votes tended to unify northern and southern Democrats.

At the same time, there is an upward trend through the 1950s. This supports an argument that as civil rights moved up the agenda, the northern-southern Democratic coalition began to fray on social welfare. After the passage of the major civil rights laws of the 1960s, the average angle of social welfare votes actually jumped well above 90 degrees. By the 1970s, social welfare had become a second-dimension issue. The likely culprit, given our results in the previous sections, is the southern Democrats voting with Republicans in opposition to liberal Democrats.

Finally, consider what happens at the end of the series. The angles now hover right around 90 degrees. In other words, today voting on social welfare breaks along a standard liberal-conservative economic dimension. Social welfare votes increasingly map onto the standard left-right economic divide.

The next question is this: What happens to civil rights? Figure 5.6 also includes a similar overtime trend of the average angle on civil rights votes by Congress. The civil rights trend line starts in the eighty-fifth Congress (1957–1958) because there were insufficient roll calls on civil and voting rights before 1957 to provide reliable estimates. At the same time that civil rights was a raging issue nationwide, it was largely kept off the congressional roll-call agenda (Schickler 2016).

In the 1950s the cutting line angles are well above 90 degrees. This is consistent with the standard narrative in which civil rights was a second-dimension issue, operating separately from support for economic liberalism (Poole and Rosenthal 1997; Schickler 2016). On one side were southern Democrats and racially conservative Republicans. On the other side were northern Democrats and racially liberal Republicans. The split did not track either partisanship or traditional economic divides. From the 1950s through the 1980s, civil rights roll-call votes consistently marched toward 90 degrees. By the end of the series, civil rights mapped onto the traditional liberal-conservative dimension – in other words, the first dimension of Congressional politics.

Thus, by the end of the twentieth century, voting on social welfare and voting on civil rights had become highly correlated. Both issues became part of the dominant liberal-conservative dimension of Congressional politics. Today, knowing a senator's ideal point on social welfare will also tell you that senator's position on civil rights. In modern American politics, support and opposition for civil rights intertwines with support and opposition for social welfare. We take this as a given in contemporary politics, but it is a dramatic departure from the New Deal politics of the 1930s and 1940s that produced dramatic progress in social welfare legislation.

CONCLUSION

In 1947, shortly after the end of World War II, the American South was not simply the most Democratic region of the country, it was also the most politically liberal measured on the basis of ADA scores. Seventy years later, it has become the most conservative region of the country, and Democratic prospects in the region are severely diminished. One might certainly protest such a statement based on the fact that racial equality had been effectively excluded from the political agenda until 1948. Indeed, New Deal liberalism had failed to advance the Second

Revolution in American Politics, brought about by the Civil War and the adoption of the Fourteenth Amendment to the US Constitution.[8] Due process, equal protection, and color-blind politics within the states were unrealized dreams, and the New Deal made only modest symbolic progress in moving the civil rights agenda forward.

The issue is really twofold. First, liberalism has been redefined and expanded to focus on issues revolving around the Fourteenth Amendment – issues of due process and equal protection without regard to race or national origin. Second, while these issues often carry economic implications – nondiscriminatory hiring practices, affirmative action programs in employment, and so on – the goals provide a different focus than the liberalism that promoted an earlier populist agenda. This earlier agenda was racially biased, and it also ignored the aspirations of women. The newer liberal agenda, in turn, has lost its widespread populist economic appeal, and it has difficulty in maintaining support among economically disadvantaged groups within the white population. Perhaps not surprisingly, this has taken place in a context where industrial trade unions are in retreat, and economic inequality has expanded within the larger population.

While progress in civil rights legislation during the 1950s and 1960s was fundamentally dependent on the collaboration and leadership of the Republican Party (Whalen and Whalen 1985; Purdum 2014), the transformation of liberalism has also produced striking changes in the nature of conservatism. The Republican party of the 1940s and 1950s was a party of individual freedom, in terms of both economic activity and civil rights. When the Democratic Party evolved into the party of civil rights, important elements of the Republican Party evolved into the party of a conservative white populist rebellion. Indeed, the southern strategy of Richard Nixon embraced southern whites disaffected by a national government and a Democratic Party that embraced the aspirations of racial minorities, cultural minorities, and women.

In short, by embracing a southern strategy that ultimately attracted major levels of support among whites, the Republican Party compromised its appeal among African Americans in the South and elsewhere. In the Deep South states like Mississippi, the Democratic candidate for

---

[8] We appropriate the title of the "Second Revolution," less in the sense of Beard and Beard (1927), but rather in the context of the post–Civil War revisions in the US Constitution to right the wrongs of slavery, the three-fifths compromise, and its failure to create a guaranteed definition of citizenship that was common and inviolable across the States (McPherson 1982, 1988, 1992).

president typically obtains more than 90 percent of the African American vote but less than 20 percent of the white vote (Huckfeldt and Kohfeld 1989: 1). And as we have seen in the country as a whole, the Democratic candidate for president has not obtained majority support among whites since 1964.

The elusive element in this contemporary political configuration is the unified representation of the economically disadvantaged population within American politics. Not only is voting in national elections structured by race, but some interests are not fully represented. A conservative Republican Party wins majority support among disadvantaged whites, while a liberal Democratic Party wins supermajority support among disadvantaged African Americans and sizeable majorities among other disadvantaged minority groups. Most discussions of the economic inequality gap in American life focus on macroeconomic change, but a close reading of American political history since the end of World War II suggests that partisan political change has played a crucial role as well.

6

Transforming the Twentieth-Century House

This chapter addresses the ideological transformation of political parties as they were represented by state delegations within the House of Representatives. So long as social welfare policy was kept separate from civil rights, it was politically feasible for southern delegations to support social welfare. The coupling of civil rights and social welfare led to a wholesale partisan realignment within the House as well as within the country as a whole.

After keeping civil rights legislation off the congressional agenda throughout the first half of the twentieth century, the dam burst and members of both parties in the House and in the Senate confronted a politically charged climate surrounding not only civil rights legislation but social welfare legislation as well. House Democrats in the South had been fully complicit in bottling up civil rights legislation while supporting social welfare legislation in the form of the New Deal and Fair Deal initiatives. Conversely, House Republicans could still make a claim to be the party of civil rights even while they adopted an economically conservative stance toward social welfare spending.

At midcentury, support for civil rights and social welfare spending became coupled, making it difficult for members of Congress to be in favor of one and opposed to the other. As we have seen in the Senate, this led to a redefinition of the political parties, not only among newly elected members but also in terms of long-time members. In particular, many southern Democrats and northern Republicans held positions on civil rights and social welfare that were incompatible in the new political environment of the post–World War II period. With political survival at stake, many of these members redefined their ideological positions on these fundamentally important issue dimensions in American politics, leading to a transformed political terrain for advocates of both civil rights and social welfare.

In this chapter we consider the political transformation of the House of Representatives. Our primary focus is on regional patterns of change among House members as they were affected by the events surrounding the adoption of civil rights legislation, as well as by the regional migration of African Americans out of the South. The analysis gives closer attention to the political dynamics within the state of Alabama against the backdrop of Key's (1949) seminal post–World War II analysis. Alabama provides a particularly important and interesting case in view of its strong populist history.

RECONSTRUCTING THE PARTIES: 1940–1954
VERSUS 1965–1979

This chapter's analysis builds on the Senate analysis of Chapter 5 for the House, using different data, employing different measurement procedures, as well as addressing an alternative measure of liberalism that expands the scope of the analysis beyond our primary concern – social welfare policy. As we have seen, the Democratic Party was fundamentally compromised in its ability to champion civil rights by its reliance on the southern delegation. None of the New Deal advances in social welfare legislation would have been possible without the party's southern wing, but this meant that the party was politically incapable of addressing the moral and constitutional issue of racial discrimination. The problem extended beyond the Senate, and this chapter considers the impact of the civil rights revolution on the evolution of American political parties as they are reflected in the House.

We begin by focusing on the voting records of US House members in 1940–1954 as compared to 1965–1979, treating the analysis as a comparison between two independent cross sections, separated in time by the events of the civil rights revolution. Our empirical strategy is to examine regional variation in the ideological locations of representatives across time. To do this, we rely on first-dimension W-nominate scores calculated on a yearly basis and including virtually all legislative votes. These data are constructed by Keith Poole and available on his website (voteview.com).

The first dimension of W-nominate captures the socioeconomic dimension of roll-call voting throughout US history, including social welfare policy (Poole and Rosenthal 1985). Hence, the first-dimension W-nominate scores provide a time-specific measure based on all the issues confronted in a particular session of the Congress. Unlike the DW-nominate scores, each year's score is independent of the previous year's score. The scores serve to index virtually every vote taken in the House, for each year and over time, and they typically produce (at most) a two-dimensional issue space – the first being a consistent measure of economic liberalism with the second dimension being an episodic, transitional dimension focused on civil rights.

The first dimension serves our purposes well. It provides a measure that is closely related to support for social welfare policy as a primary aspect of liberal economic policy but independent from civil rights. Hence, we are able to consider this more broadly based economic dimension – closely related to social welfare policy but independent from civil rights support – as it may be contingent on the political events taking place relative to the civil rights movement in American politics during the 1950s and 1960s. Moreover, this provides the opportunity to consider whether the problem of race extends more generally to the larger liberal agenda.[1]

As in the previous analyses, the cardinal values of W-nominate scores are not directly comparable over time, and thus we rank-ordered representatives in each year and then converted these rank orderings into percentiles. The most liberal members in a session are at the 1st percentile, the median at the 50th percentile, and the most conservative at the 100th percentile. Examining the ordered rankings of representatives has a number of appealing modeling advantages. Because the underlying ideological scale in any given session is unobserved, cardinal comparisons between representatives are sensitive to the distribution of proposals brought to the floor (Ho and Quinn 2010). By contrast, ordinal comparisons are less vulnerable to variation in the distribution of proposals and cut points. As such, finding movement in the relative ordinal rankings of legislators over time provides a strong evidence of change (Ho and Quinn 2010: 846).

---

[1] The primary alternative scaling method to W-nominate scores are DW-nominate scores. These scores also take into account the roll-call record of a member's entire career, but the disadvantage for our purposes is that changes in DW-nominate ideal points are constrained to change in a linear fashion. Using rank-ordered W-nominate scores, by contrast, allows for ideal points to move in an arbitrary fashion over time and year by year, in response to political conditions and events as they unfold.

Once again, changes in a member's ordinal ranking may be due to at least two processes. First, members may shift their ideal points. Second, replacement in the rest of the chamber may alter a member's ordinal ranking. For example, the entry of a large batch of liberal members who replace conservatives will push the rank orders of moderates further to the right; even if moderates did not change their underlying ideal point. We present a sensitivity analysis here showing that southern representatives moved rightward much faster than member replacement would suggest.

One might, of course, employ the measures we have used previously – ADA scores for House members or the W-nominate scores we constructed for social welfare votes alone. The goal in this chapter is somewhat different. Our aim is to demonstrate the far-reaching consequences of the populist failure to construct a lower-class movement that incorporates all racial groups within a larger coalition broadly representing the interests of working-class and lower-middle-class citizens. The political implications extend beyond civil rights and social welfare, with consequences for the entire liberal agenda in American politics. Hence, the W-nominate scores provide a measure that is directly relevant to the argument we are making.

POLITICAL CHANGE IN THE HOUSE

Table 6.1 provides a simple descriptive comparison of the House membership by region between these two time periods. First, Part A shows the political composition of the regional House delegations. New England, the Atlantic, the Midwest, and the Pacific states show substantial increases in the percentage of Democratic members. Democratic losses are concentrated in the South and, to a lesser extent in the mountain states, and they are much less substantial overall. Indeed, the 1965–1979 period includes the high watermark for Democratic ascendancy, and Democratic dominance begins to decline in the 1980s and thereafter.

Part B of Table 6.1 considers the regional variation of House member rankings on W-nominate during the two periods. During the pre–civil rights period, the most liberal scores occur among the southern delegation, where the predicted rank is the 38th percentile (0.75–0.37). During the latter period, after the civil rights revolution, the most conservative scores occur among the southern delegation, where the predicted rank is the 67th percentile (0.70–0.03). In contrast, New England's predicted

TABLE 6.1. *Race, civil rights, and the evolution of American politics*

A. The changing political party profile by region

1940–1954	New England	Atlantic	Border	South	Midwest	Plains	Mountain	Pacific	Total
Dem.%	33.17	41.51	72.78	97.34	27.04	6.05	59.74	43.72	53.56
Rep.%	66.83	57.46	27.22	2.53	71.54	93.95	40.26	56.28	45.85
N	419	1,354	632	1,543	1,553	215	231	494	6,441

1965–1979	New England	Atlantic	Border	South	Midwest	Plains	Mountain	Pacific	Total
Dem.%	64.03	61.71	74.68	75.39	46.75	15.61	51.67	62.55	61.26
Rep.%	35.42	38.29	25.32	24.61	53.25	84.39	48.33	37.45	38.71
N	367	1,217	545	1,605	1,523	173	269	769	6,468

(continued)

TABLE 6.1 *(continued)*

B. The changing ideological profile by region, measured by the House members' percentile rank on the first dimension of W-nominate, where 0 is the most liberal and 1 is the most conservative. Regions are dummy-coded with the plains states as the excluded baseline

	1940–1954			1965–1979		
	Coefficient	Standard Error	*t*-Ratio	Coefficient	Standard Error	*t*-Ratio
New England	–0.22	0.02	–9.67	–0.39	0.02	–16.10
Atlantic	–0.27	0.02	–13.71	–0.34	0.02	–15.81
Border	–0.33	0.02	–15.59	–0.20	0.02	–8.95
South	–0.37	0.02	–18.70	–0.03	0.02	–1.24
Midwest	–0.11	0.02	–5.82	–0.20	0.02	–9.69
Mountain	–0.28	0.03	–11.12	–0.10	0.03	–4.07
Pacific	–0.27	0.02	–12.37	–0.29	0.02	–13.37
Constant	0.75	0.02	40.72	0.70	0.02	35.01

$R^2 = 0.13$
SE (est.) = 0.27
N = 6440

$R^2 = 0.19$
SE (est.) = 0.26
N = 646

rank is 0.53 (0.75–0.22) during the earlier period and 0.41 (0.70–0.39) in the latter period. In short, the changes in ideological rank considerably outstrip the changes in partisan composition.

This analysis suggests that the changes occurring are not simply due to changes in the partisan divisions within the House but are more fundamentally due to ideological changes that are occurring within the House party memberships – that is, to a fundamental ideological redefinition of the parties. Table 6.1 provides only a simple analysis of the changes that were underway, and hence, we turn to a more complete analysis employing difference-in-differences estimators.

IDEOLOGICAL CHANGE BY REGION

Table 6.2 extends the analysis in Table 6.1 to provide a direct estimate of the effects due to the civil rights revolution on the regional distribution of House members' ideological rankings. As before, we generate regional estimates of the members' percentile rankings on W-nominate, but in this analysis, the pre–civil rights and post–civil rights revolution periods are pooled, with dummy variables to represent regions as well as the two time periods. Dummy variables are also included to provide interaction measures of the regionally specific time effects and the temporally specific regional effects. In short, this framework allows a direct joint comparison of time and space relative to the political implications of the civil rights revolution. We employ robust standard errors clustered by states, but in several instances, we cluster smaller states with similar adjacent states to maintain n-sizes within clusters: Delaware with Maryland, Nevada with Utah, North Dakota with South Dakota, New Mexico with Arizona, and Wyoming with Montana.

Table 6.3 employs the results from Table 6.2 to examine the effect on the percentile W-nominate rankings within regions as well as each region's distance from the median (50th percentile) ranking. The largest changes in rank orderings occur among the New England states and the South. The South moves from a rank order in the 39th percentile to the 68th percentile, while New England moves from the 54th percentile to the 32nd percentile and the Atlantic states move from the 48th percentile to the 37th percentile.

All three regions also move farther away from the median. During the earlier period, New England and the Atlantic regions were both statistically indistinguishable from the median, but they became the most

TABLE 6.2. *Regional difference-in-differences estimators for percentile rankings on first-dimension ideological scores in the US House, 1940–1954 versus 1965–1979*

	Coefficient	Standard Error	t-Value	
New England	−0.20	0.083	2.43	
Middle Atlantic	−0.26	0.046	5.66	
Border	−0.33	0.048	5.91	
South	−0.36	0.042	8.41	
Midwest	−0.11	0.044	2.42	$N = 12,909$
Mountain West	−0.26	0.079	3.31	$R^2 = 0.16$
Pacific	−0.26	0.061	4.27	
Y65-79	−0.05	0.018	2.81	
New England × Y65-79	−0.17	0.047	3.62	
Atlantic × Y65-79	−0.06	0.028	2.31	
Border × Y65-79	0.13	0.050	2.53	
South × Y65-79	0.34	0.031	11.04	
Midwest × Y65-79	−0.09	0.033	2.81	
Mountain × Y65-79	−0.18	0.010	1.81	
Pacific × Y65-79	0.03	0.028	0.90	
Constant	0.74	0.040	18.43	

Note: Rankings are on a scale from most liberal (0) to most conservative (1). Regions are dummy-coded, with plains states as the excluded baseline. Y65-79 = 1 if an observation is between 1965 and 1979, inclusive; 0 if it is between 1940 and 1954, inclusive.

The analysis is clustered by states, with the six smallest states combined with neighboring states: Delaware with Maryland, Nevada with Utah, North Dakota with South Dakota, New Mexico with Arizona, and Wyoming with Montana. The dependent variable is the member's percentile ranking on the first-dimension W-nominate score. Hawaii and Alaska are excluded because they did not achieve statehood until after the first period was over. Hence, the number of clusters is 42, with a minimum of observations per cluster of 60, a maximum of 1,262, and an average of 307.4.

Regions:
New England: Six states – CT, MA, ME, NH, RI, VT
Middle Atlantic: Three states – NY, PA, NJ
Border: Six states – DE, KT, MD, MO, WV, OK
South: Eleven states – TX, AR, LA, MS, AL, TN, GA, SC, NC, VA, FL
Midwest: Seven states – IA, MN, WI, MI, IL, IN, OH
Plains: Four states – ND, SD, NE, KS
Mountain West: Eight states – MT, ID, WY, UT, CO, AZ, NM, NV
Pacific: Three states – WA, OR, CA

TABLE 6.3. *Predicted percentile ranks and proximity to the median for first dimension regional estimates in the US House, 1940–1954 and 1965–1979*

	Percentile Rank			Distance from Median		
	1940s	1990s	Difference	1940s	1990s	Difference
New England	0.54	0.32	−0.22	0.06	0.18	0.12
Atlantic	0.48	0.37	−0.11	0.02	0.13	0.11
Border	0.41	0.49	0.08	0.09	0.01	−0.08
South	0.39	0.68	0.29	0.11	0.18	0.07
Midwest	0.49	0.49	0	0.01	0.01	0
Plains	0.74	0.69	−0.05	0.26	0.15	−0.08
Mountain	0.48	0.61	0.13	0.02	0.16	0.10
Pacific	0.48	0.41	0.08	0.02	0.06	0.04

Note: Ranking is on a scale from most liberal (0) to most conservative (1).

liberal stalwarts. The South moved from the most liberal to being tied with the plains states as the most conservative. In short, the liberal mantle passed from the South to the Northeast.

IDEOLOGICAL CHANGE BY REGION AND PARTY

While the analysis has shown important changes by region, our goal is to show changes within parties. In this context, Table 6.4 examines the effect of time on the ideological positions of Democrats by region, and these results are translated into predicted rank orders and distance from the median in Table 6.5. The table shows the largest changes in the southern, midwestern, and mountain regions. Southern Democrats move from the 38th percentile rank to the 62nd percentile rank. Mountain Democrats move from the 25th percentile rank to the 42nd. And the Midwest moves from the 49th percentile rank to the 22nd.

These results point to the fact that after the civil rights revolution, the liberal wing of the liberal party became anchored in the New England, Atlantic, Midwest, and Pacific regions. The border and southern Democrats have moved toward or beyond the median ideological position of the House as a whole – the border Democrats lie 9 points below the median and the southern Democrats lie 12 points above the median. In short, the heart and soul of the Democratic Party has been displaced to the Northeast, and the Southern wing of the party is steadily moving toward the conservative end of the ideological spectrum.

TABLE 6.4. *Regional difference-in-differences estimators among Democratic House members for percentile rankings on first-dimension ideological scores, 1940–1954 to 1965–1979*

	Coefficient	Standard Error	t-Value	
New England	−0.19	0.05	3.90	
Middle Atlantic	−0.27	0.04	7.03	
Border	−0.14	0.04	3.44	
South	−0.04	0.04	0.99	
Midwest	−0.23	0.04	5.04	$N = 7,412$
Mountain West	−0.17	0.04	3.78	$R^2 = 0.47$
Pacific	−0.16	0.05	3.03	
1970s	−0.07	0.03	1.99	
New England × Y65-79	0.05	0.05	1.14	
Atlantic × Y65-79	0.13	0.04	3.49	
Border × Y65-79	0.20	0.05	4.09	
South × Y65-79	0.31	0.04	7.08	
Midwest × Y65-79	0.10	0.04	2.39	
Mountain × Y65-79	0.24	0.06	3.85	
Pacific × Y65-79	0.05	0.05	1.02	
Constant	0.42	0.04	11.23	

Note: Rankings are on a scale from most liberal (0) to most conservative (1). Regions are dummy-coded, with the plains states as the excluded baseline.

Y65-79 = 1 if an observation is between 1965 and 1979, inclusive; 0 if it is between 1940 and 1954, inclusive.

The analysis is clustered by states, with the six smallest states combined with neighboring states: Delaware with Maryland, Nevada with Utah, North Dakota with South Dakota, New Mexico with Arizona, and Wyoming with Montana. The dependent variable is the member's percentile ranking on the first-dimension W-nominate score. Hawaii and Alaska are excluded because they did not achieve statehood until after the first period was over. Hence, the number of clusters is 42, with a minimum of observations per cluster of 7, a maximum of 696, and an average of 176.5.

Tables 6.6 and 6.7 carry out a comparable analysis for the Republicans. In general the results show that New England and Middle Atlantic Republicans move toward the liberal end of the scale, and the southern Republicans move toward the conservative end of the scale. This movement reflects the general regional trends, with the Northeast becoming more liberal and the South becoming more conservative. Hence, the results in Tables 6.4–6.7 suggest a pattern in which ideological change within regions is not simply a matter of party replacement within the House. To the contrary, regional ideological considerations are reflected within the parties as well as between them.

TABLE 6.5. *Predicted percentile ranks and proximity to the median for first-dimension regional estimates among Democrats in the US House, 1940–1954 and 1965–1979*

	Percentile Rank			Distance from Median		
	1940s	1970s	Difference	1940s	1970s	Difference
New England	0.23	0.21	−0.02	0.27	0.29	0.02
Atlantic	0.15	0.21	0.06	0.35	0.29	−0.06
Border	0.27	0.41	0.13	0.23	0.09	−0.14
South	0.38	0.62	0.24	0.12	0.12	0
Midwest	0.49	0.22	−0.27	0.01	0.28	0.27
Plains	0.42	0.35	−0.07	0.08	0.15	0.07
Mountain	0.25	0.42	0.17	0.25	0.18	−0.13
Pacific	0.26	0.24	−0.02	0.24	0.26	0.02

Note: Ranking is from most liberal (0) to most conservative (1).

TABLE 6.6. *Regional difference-in-differences estimators among Republican House members for percentile rankings on first-dimension ideological scores, 1940–1954 to 1965–1979*

	Coefficient	Standard Error	t-Value	
New England	−0.07	0.05	1.32	
Middle Atlantic	−0.05	0.05	0.89	
Border	0.02	0.05	0.32	
South	−0.05	0.05	0.99	
Midwest	0.03	0.05	0.65	$N = 5457$
Mountain West	0.02	0.06	0.37	$R^2 = 0.18$
Pacific	−0.10	0.05	1.98	
1970s	−0.01	0.03	0.39	
New England × Y65-79	−0.18	0.06	2.99	
Atlantic × Y65-79	−0.10	0.03	3.21	
Border × Y65-79	−0.01	0.06	0.11	
South × Y65-79	0.16	0.03	5.61	
Midwest × Y65-79	−0.06	0.04	1.63	
Mountain × Y65-79	0.01	0.03	0.28	
Pacific × Y65-79	0.04	0.04	1.14	
Constant	0.77	0.05	15.63	

Note: Rankings are on a scale from most liberal (0) to most conservative (1). Regions are dummy-coded, with the plains states as the excluded baseline. Y65-79 = 1 if an observation is between 1965 and 1979, inclusive; 0 if it is between 1940 and 1954, inclusive.

Note: The analysis is clustered by states, with the six smallest states combined with neighboring states: Delaware with Maryland, Nevada with Utah, North Dakota with South Dakota, New Mexico with Arizona, and Wyoming with Montana. The dependent variable is the member's percentile ranking on the first-dimension W-nominate score. Hawaii and Alaska are excluded because they did not achieve statehood until after the first period was over. Hence, the number of clusters is 42, with a minimum of observations per cluster of 2, a maximum of 552, and an average of 129.9.

TABLE 6.7. *Predicted percentile ranks and proximity to the median for first-dimension regional estimates among Republicans in the US House, 1940–1954 and 1965–1979*

	Percentile Rank			Distance from Median		
	1940s	*1970s*	Difference	*1940s*	*1970s*	Difference
New England	0.70	0.51	−0.19	0.20	0.49	0.19
Atlantic	0.72	0.60	−0.12	0.28	0.40	0.12
Border	0.78	0.78	0	0.22	0.22	0
South	0.72	0.87	0.15	0.28	0.13	−0.15
Midwest	0.80	0.74	−0.06	0.30	0.24	−0.06
Plains	0.77	0.76	−0.01	0.23	0.24	0.01
Mountain	0.79	0.79	0	0.21	0.21	0
Pacific	0.66	0.69	0.03	0.34	0.31	0

Note: Ranking is on a scale from most conservative (0) to most liberal (1).

RECONSTRUCTING THE RACIAL AND
PARTISAN ORDER IN ALABAMA

In his path-breaking work on southern politics, Key (1949) demonstrates the importance of race-based politics and the implications of one-party control for the rise of factional politics. One of his most compelling analyses addresses populist politics in Alabama. He shows that in areas of the state where poor whites were in the majority and blacks were relatively few, politics did revolve around not *only* the politics of racial supremacy but also issues of white populist rebellion. Governor "Big Jim" Folsom and his successors undertook a style of politics inspired by class as well as race. They either embraced or were careful to avoid disrupting the repressive racial order of white supremacy, but they also supported social welfare measures that might or might not be color-blind. In contrast, the committed white supremacists, located in the so-called black belt of Alabama, were more likely to oppose any social welfare legislation.

We update Key's analysis of Alabama politics to include the following five decades. As Figure 6.1 shows, a fairly consistent pattern occurs across all the southern states' House delegations from 1940 through 1998, in which the mean percentile ranking for the state starts on the liberal side of the median, increases (sometimes dramatically), and then stabilizes at a more conservative level. In short, the civil rights revolution produced a more conservative block of representatives coming from the southern states.

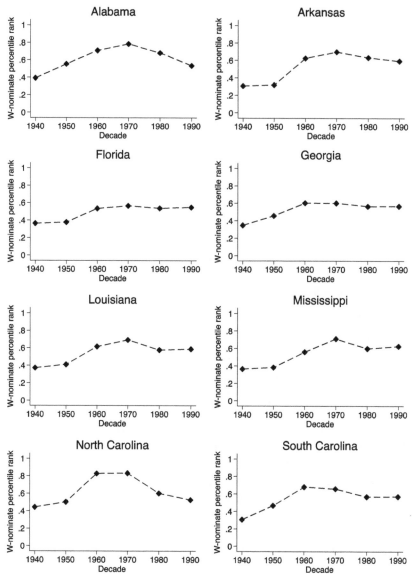

FIGURE 6.1. Mean percentile rank on first dimension of W-nominate for House members from southern states, by decade.

(continued)

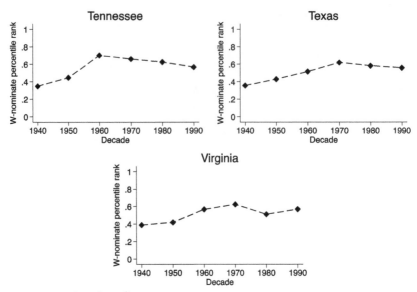

FIGURE 6.1 *(continued)*

Within this general context, we address the changing behavior of individual Alabama House members confronted by the possibility of improving social and political circumstances among African Americans. Figure 6.2 shows two plots: one for the percentile rankings of all Alabama members of the US House of Representatives from 1940 to 1998 and one for Alabama House members who served for fifteen years or more. The LOWESS curves show the strong conservative adjustment that occurs in the late 1960s, followed by a modest shift back toward the median beginning in the early 1970s. The plot for all Alabama House members shows a small cluster of liberal scores in the late 1990s. This is due to the creation of a majority-minority district in Birmingham in the latter half of the 1990s in response to the Supreme Court decision in *Thornburgh v. Gingles* and the ongoing struggle for meaningful voting rights (Bond 1990; Kousser 1974, 1999, 2008).

Figure 6.3 shows the rank-ordered W-nominate scores for each of the US House members from Alabama who served fifteen years or more during the 1940–1998 period. The plots are ordered by time, and hence, the earliest plots are all for Democrats: Grant, Andrews, Rains, Jones,

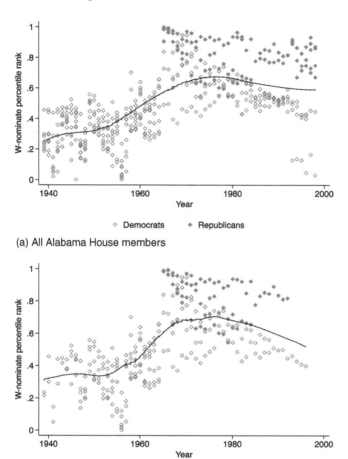

(a) All Alabama House members

(b) Alabama House members serving fifteen years or more

FIGURE 6.2. Ideological evolution of the Alabama House delegation, 1940–1998.

Elliott, and Selden. Four of the members have scores that begin below the median but trend upward, ending above the median: Grant, Andrews, Jones, and Selden. The other two, Rains and Elliott, start below the median and stay below the median. In short, we see not simply replacement but individual change as well – a process in which some but not all of the Democrats run for cover by pursuing a more conservative political agenda in their votes.

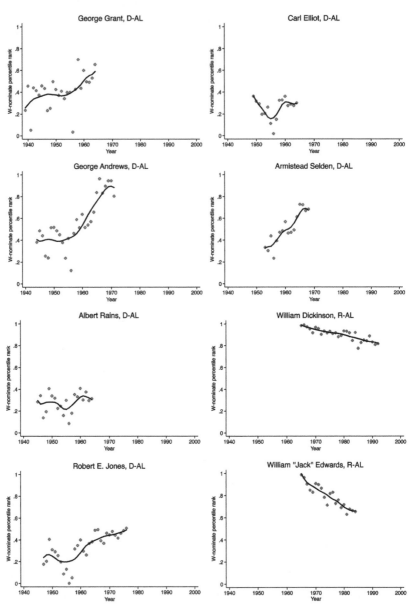

FIGURE 6.3. Ideological evolution for individual members of Alabama House delegation serving at least twenty years between 1940 and 1998.

(continued)

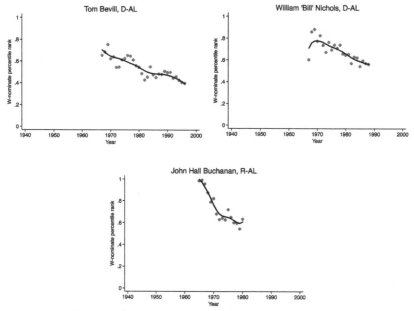

FIGURE 6.3 *(continued)*

In the late 1960s, Republicans make their entry into the Alabama House delegation: Dickinson, Edwards, and Buchanan. All three of these members start out with perfectly consistent conservative voting records, but they all moderate rather quickly so that their W-nominate scores place them at approximately the 60th percentile – on the conservative side of the median but much more moderate than when they began. Two Democrats are elected in the late 1960s as well: Bevill and Nichols. They too start out quite conservative, but not as conservative as the Republicans, and they also moderate their positions. Bevill ends up as a moderate on the liberal side of the median, and Nichols ends up as a moderate on the conservative side of the median.

THE MODERN LEGACY OF THE CIVIL
RIGHTS REALIGNMENT

In short, we see evidence at both the aggregate and individual levels that House members adjusted their ideological positions and voting records in response to the mood and tenor of the new political era. In the Northeast, the Democrats became more liberal. In the South, many

Democrats became more conservative, and many of them ended up being replaced by Republicans who ran as extreme conservatives but adopted a somewhat more moderate stance during their time in office.

Democratic members of the southern congressional delegation, both senators and House members, who had been notable for their strongly populist inclinations as well as for their strong support of liberal New Deal programs, went into full retreat. They changed their positions on the ideological issues of the day, and we see these changes in the first-dimension W-nominate percentile rankings among the southern House Democrats, as well as in ADA scores among the southern Senate Democrats. While many of these Democrats were ultimately replaced by Republicans, the first stage in the political realignment came not simply in terms of opposition to civil rights but also in terms of southern Democrats who deserted the party's social welfare agenda. If social welfare legislation was to be race neutral, southern Democrats were exiting the social welfare coalition, even if that meant deserting their populist roots.

The legacy of the partisan inversions of the 1960s and 1970s continue into the present. To see this, Figure 6.4 shows the mean percentile rankings by region for the 114th Congress (2015–2016).[2] The sharp regional differences within the House are clearly visible. The most conservative regions in 2015–2016 were the Plains, the Mountain West, and the South. The most liberal regions are now found primarily on the Pacific and Atlantic coasts. The conservative shift of the South is among the most dramatic of the regional changes. In 1948 the mean rank of southern House members was 31. Indeed, it ranked as the most liberal region of the country based on DW-nominate scores. In 2016 the mean rank of southern House members was 62. Only the plains region ranked more conservative.

Figure 6.5 shows the mean percentile rankings for each of the separate southern states. In 2015–2016 all the southern state delegations reside to the right of the House median, some by a wide margin. Consider again the example of Alabama. In recent years the Alabama House delegation ranked among the most conservative. With the exception of the Democratic district in Birmingham, the rest of the delegation is today decidedly conservative. In 2016, the Alabama delegation's mean percentile ranking was 69. In 1948 it had been 22, making it one of the more liberal delegations at the time.

---

[2] Due to data availability for the contemporary era, this figure uses DW-nominate scores.

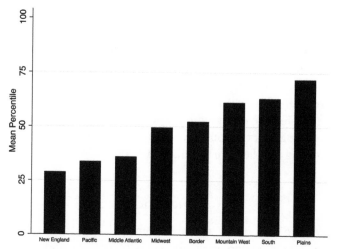

FIGURE 6.4. Regional ideological distribution in the US House, 2015–2016.

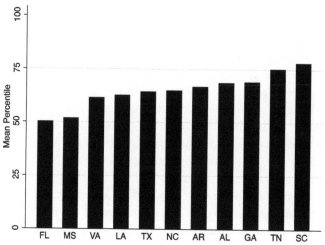

FIGURE 6.5. Ideological distribution among southern House members, 2015–2016.

These regional shifts have led to several outcomes: a Congress and a population that are more politically polarized, and a unified conservative movement that has been empowered by increased levels of support, particularly from the South. This shift was perhaps nowhere more apparent than in the approach toward health care. For instance, Senator Lister Hill (D) of Alabama cosponsored the Hill-Burton Act of 1946, which called for the construction and broad expansion of health-care facilities throughout the country. Seventy years later House Republicans from Alabama led the effort to dismantle the ACA.[3]

CONCLUSION

The decoupling of social welfare from civil rights may be difficult to imagine for contemporary observers of politics and policy in the American context. That is, however, exactly the premise upon which the New Deal's social welfare legislation was realized. As long as the South was able to maintain its own version of racial apartheid, the expansion of social welfare benefits for economically disadvantaged whites became a thriving political agenda among the southern populists who were crucial supporters of Roosevelt and his New Deal.

In his analysis of southern politics, V. O. Key argued that the 1948 Dixiecrat revolt might have been the "dying gasp" (1949: 671) of the old South – a revolt that he ascribed to whites in the "black belt" counties together with "their entourage of professional Ku Kluxers, antidiluvian reactionaries, and malodorous opportunists" (1949: 10). Quite clearly, even the insightful Key underestimated the staying power of race and racial politics in America.

Not only did race overtake the populist movement in southern politics, but in doing so, it led to a realignment of the national political parties. As southern whites rebelled against the enforcement of the Fourteenth Amendment and the expansion of citizenship rights for African Americans, the Southern wing of the Democratic party in Congress pulled back its support for social welfare legislation. Undoubtedly, the southerners were running scared, and their shifting positions on social welfare policy reflected their fears of being seen as accommodating toward the African American population. In time most

---

[3] www.nytimes.com/2015/02/04/us/politics/house-gop-again-votes-to-repeal-health-care-law.html

of these Democrats would be replaced by conservative Republicans, but the regionally based realignment had already occurred.

It would be an enormous mistake to underestimate the importance of the welfare state's significant expansion accomplished by Franklin Roosevelt and the New Deal Democratic Party during the 1930s, 1940s, and early 1950s. The Fair Labor Standards Act and the Social Security Act, in particular, still provide the foundation upon which much of the American social welfare state has been constructed. Indeed, it is difficult to imagine the current state of American social welfare policy absent these events.

At the same time, it would also be a mistake to ignore the deal with the devil that made these events possible. The political reality of the 1930s and 1940s was that nothing could be accomplished without the support of the southern Democratic delegations in the House and Senate. And the price of their collaboration was that the social welfare state and its benefits must operate within the discriminatory practices that excluded African Americans from participation, at least in the South (Katznelson 2013). If blacks were to be included in the benefits, southern support disappeared even if that meant the loss of benefits for whites as well.

The civil rights revolution changed all this, and the last great accomplishment of the New Deal legacy was the adoption of Medicare, Medicaid, and the rest of Johnson's Great Society legislation during the 1960s. While the Great Society initiative and its programs have mostly disappeared, Medicare and Medicaid continue, but progress on further expansions have been slow in coming and remain under threat.

The tortured history of the ACA illustrates the contemporary version of the problem. Many groups in American society benefit from the health care coverage provided by the Veteran's Administration and Medicare, but many who are receiving these benefits are opposed to any expansion of this coverage to disadvantaged groups. In short, the distinction between worthy and unworthy recipients of social welfare programs has continued (Piven and Cloward 1971), where the unworthy are likely to be defined as those unlike the person who is offering the evaluation (Frederico 2004; Gilens 1996).

We should not be surprised at this state of affairs. In the early twentieth century, Sombart (1906) asked his famous question, "Why is there no socialism in the United States?" He offered a number of answers to his own question, but the answer that has the most enduring purchase is the racial and ethnic diversity of the American population.

Our focus is not on socialism but rather on the provision of social welfare benefits that are common to other advanced capitalist democracies. Quite clearly, the vast majority of Americans support Medicaid and Social Security, which combine to produce a third rail in American politics. At the same time, a majority of white Americans resist an expansion of social welfare benefits, such as the ACA. The history of American politics suggests that social welfare benefits are more likely to be supported if the beneficiaries are members of the supporters' own social groups. Homogeneous European societies realized a distinct advantage in the establishment and maintenance of their own social welfare system. In the current era, these same European democracies are beginning to realize problems similar to those of the United States. Particularly within the context of free migration within the Eurozone, one might wonder whether the achievements of the European social welfare state could be duplicated in the current context.

Once again, we wholly endorse Poole's (2005) argument that democratic politics has great difficulty accommodating more than one primary policy dimension. At the same time, we would qualify the argument (Poole 2007) that individual politicians never change their positions. In the House as in the Senate, however, we see clear evidence of individual politicians changing their roll-call voting behavior when policy dimensions come into conflict. While they may not change their true underlying preferences, those preferences adapt to the political winds. And hence, when policy dimensions come into conflict, the pressure will often be intense for politicians to adjust their positions on one dimension or the other. In the context of the civil rights revolution, this meant that southern Democrats who had always endorsed white supremacy felt compelled to adopt a more conservative position on social welfare issues. In contrast, pro–civil rights Republican moderates were frequently compelled to adopt more liberal social and economic positions with respect to social welfare policy.

Conservative Republicans ultimately replaced many of these dissenting Democrats, and many dissenting Republicans were ultimately replaced by liberal Democrats. This does not change the fact, however, that individual change led to the realignment. A continuing challenge for American politics is to disentangle the relationship between social welfare and racial hostility, and progress on this front ultimately depends on changing attitudes and opinions among American voters.

7

Race, Class, and a Transformed Political Economy

Turning Populism Upside Down

We won with the poorly educated. I love the poorly educated.

—Donald Trump[1]

Democrats blew the opportunity the American people gave them [in 2008]....Only a third of the uninsured are even registered to vote. In 2010 only about 40 percent of those registered voted. So even if the uninsured kept with the rate, which they likely did not, we would still only be talking about only 5 percent of the electorate. To aim a huge change in mandate at such a small percentage of the electorate made no political sense.

—Senator Charles Schumer[2]

The contemporary versions of the major political coalitions in American politics demonstrate an attenuated relationship with the parties as they existed at the end of the 1940s, or even at the beginning of the 1960s. The transformation has certainly been less than complete. The Democratic Party continues to be closely associated with the mantle of liberalism, while the Republican Party continues to embrace conservative values and political positions across a wide range of issues. At a more profound level, however, the class and racial alignments of the parties have been radically transformed over the past sixty years, and liberalism and conservatism have taken on different meanings.

---

[1] Elizabeth Williamson. "A Big Win for Donald Trump in Nevada," *New York Times*, February 24, 2016. Trump's comment came after winning the Nevada GOP caucus.
[2] Thomas Edsall, "Is Obamacare Destroying the Democratic Party?" *New York Times*, December 22, 2015. Comments made at a National Press Club speech on November 25, 2014.

As the previous chapters demonstrated, one central element of this transformation was the civil rights revolution in American politics. Race and civil rights do not, however, provide a complete account. Other important changes were occurring at the same time, with important consequences for the alignment of American political parties. The end result has been an overall decline in the class basis of the party coalitions. This decline is not simply due to a reduced rate at which working-class voters support the Democratic Party. More importantly, working-class occupations have declined dramatically as a percentage of the electorate, while professional and managerial occupations have increased. Moreover, professional and managerial occupations have increased their level of support for the Democrats. This transformation of the class basis of the parties has generated far-reaching implications for the composition of party coalitions, the organizational base of party support, and the commitment of the Democratic Party to social welfare measures.

THE NEW ECOLOGY OF PARTY SUPPORT

The racial divide is not, of course, the only source of conflict in American politics, and the role of race is best understood relative to these other sources of political conflict and competition. In particular, social class and regional boundaries continue to provide primary boundaries structuring interest aggregation within American politics. While the civil rights struggles have generated important progress along a number of fronts, they also coincided with the creation of a political environment that is in some ways less congenial to extensions of the social welfare state in American politics.

This problem is perhaps best illustrated in the context of the South, where support for social welfare legislation evaporated once the benefits were to be shared equally, on a nondiscriminatory basis for blacks as well as whites. Once social welfare liberalism was associated with civil rights liberalism and an extension of benefits to nonwhites, support for social welfare declined. A common reaction among racially biased whites was racial resentment and an unwillingness to support any candidate or party that provided support and benefits to blacks (see Jardina 2019).

One response is to blame the problem on people who might be expected to support social welfare legislation if, in fact, they voted on the basis of their own class-based interests. Indeed, many of these issues have been addressed by Frank (2004), who blames the voters who would be the primary beneficiaries of social welfare benefits yet vote in ways that would appear to be contrary to their own best interests. While Bartels (2006, 2008) identifies a series of problems with Frank's analysis, his own collaborative analyses of the electorate's limited powers of discernment (Achen and Bartels 2016) point toward the limited capacity of voters to puzzle through a reasonable calculation of their own best interests.

Our goal in this chapter is to assess the changing basis of party support and the implications for party politics going forward. Working-class politics has been historically central to the extension of social welfare benefits. At the same time, working-class movements are often quite difficult to sustain, and this fact is highlighted in Sombart's (1976) early consideration of the conspicuous absence of socialism in the United States at a time when it was flourishing in Europe. As Sombart recognized, a variety of factors carry the potential to derail working-class movements and social democratic parties, mostly having to do with competing factors that fracture working-class cohesion.

THE POLITICAL DECLINE OF THE WORKING CLASS

Perhaps the most compelling evidence regarding the political decline of the working class is that politicians seldom use the phrase. Seventy years ago, the Congress of Industrial Organizations (CIO) was the primary basis of organizational support for Franklin Roosevelt's electoral coalition, and mobilizing the "working class" was a primary component of the Democratic Party vocabulary. Thirty years ago, Democratic politicians would still regularly address problems faced by the "working class," but the working-class label has since fallen out of favor, having been abandoned in favor of an appeal to a more heterogeneous and perhaps more respectable "middle class." For example, Bernie Sanders sometimes employs the working-class label, but his 2016 candidate website posted an official position on "Income and Wealth Inequality" that refers only to the "middle class" and the "poor," absent any mention of the "working class."

At the same time, the evidence does not suggest that the phrase has necessarily fallen out of fashion as a label of self-identification among the general public. Using the National Election Study Series, Hout (2008) shows that approximately 60 percent of the sample self-identified as some category of working class in 1956, 64 percent in 1960, 51 percent in 2004, and 53 percent in 2008. In short, approximately half the sample continues to self-identify as working class – a relatively modest decline in the frequency of working-class identification from the mid-twentieth to the early twenty-first century. As we will see, the relatively modest decline in self-identification is not necessarily status driven and might instead be seen as a reflection of demographic and economic change within American society. Our argument is that the decline of class in American electoral politics has less to do with self-identification and more to do with politics, demographics, and political organization.

DEFINING SOCIAL CLASS

The literature on social class and electoral change within the white population has focused on various measures of social standing. Bartels (2006) offers a review of several options that have been employed, and his own analysis makes use of income class (also see Stonecash 2000). Other analysts recommend the use of education (Abramowitz and Teixeira 2009), and our own efforts primarily employ occupational class as a measure of individuals' shared circumstances within the larger political economy. In Hout's (2008: 26) words, class provides a measure of "how people make their money" and thus taps into their "shared interests." In this sense, the teller at a bank branch may have more in common, in both political and aspirational terms, with the well-paid MBA who is the bank manager rather than with a similarly paid individual working in a factory as a machine operator's helper (Przeworski and Sprague 1986: Chapter 2).

Bartels (2006) finds no change in the effect of income on the vote, while Abramowitz and Teixeira (2009) find that people with lower levels of education have become less likely to support Democratic candidates. We have no reason, either substantive or theoretical, to doubt these results or the scholarship that produced them. Our own effort defines class in terms of occupational status, but we are not necessarily arguing that it is a better measure of class, but rather a more useful one for our purposes. In particular, it provides several substantive advantages.

First, in terms of face validity, we argue that occupational categories provide a measure that is related to *membership in a group* rather than a measure of individual attainment. Individual attainment – education or income – is, of course, related to group membership in important ways, but there are important differences as well. In particular, occupational categories have a great deal to do with social interaction patterns

(Carnes 2013). The clerk at a bank is likely to interact with bankers, while a similarly paid and educated blue-collar worker in a factory is likely to interact with other blue-collar workers. These patterns of interaction carry important implications for political communication of preferences, the mix of political messages, and patterns of interdependence within electorates (Huckfeldt and Sprague 1995). The important point is that public opinion is not only a consequence of what happens between the ears of voters as a consequence of news reports and campaign appeals. It is also a direct consequence of group-based patterns of interdependence among voters, and this is especially true regarding group boundaries based on race, ethnicity, and class (Huckfeldt and Kohfeld 1989).

Second, the occupational categories employed by the American National Election Study (ANES) are based on US Census categories that are comparable across time.[3] Hence, we consider the behavior of individuals within these categories across time, but we also consider the change in the parties' level of reliance on particular groups across time, as well as the growth and decline of the groups both within the electorate and within the larger population. *In other words, there is more than one way that the Democratic Party can lose its white working-class base.* White workers might quit voting for the party; or the level of support for the party might stay constant within the group, but the size of the group might have decreased; or the size of the group in the electorate might decline because the group size has changed relative to the larger population. Any of these scenarios carry the potential to transform the composition of the party coalition as well as the political appeal to voters that the party constructs.

CHANGING LEVELS OF DEMOCRATIC SUPPORT AMONG WHITE OCCUPATIONAL GROUPS

We begin by considering the proportion of the eligible electorate supporting Democratic presidential candidates across time, region, race, and occupational class. Our initial focus is on Democratic support relative to the base of all eligible voters rather than to the base of just those who voted, in order to take into account turnout levels within the groups. At the same time, it is important to remember that overreports of turnout are endemic to survey recall data.

---

[3] Occupational data are not readily available in the ANES after 2004. We augment the analysis by also examining party support across educational categories. This supplementary analysis can be found in Appendix 7.A.

Figure 7.1 shows the level of Democratic mobilization – the proportion of the eligible population voting Democratic – as a function of occupational class, defined relative to the respondent's reported occupation for the nation as a whole, as well as for the Northeast and the South. For these purposes we define the working class in terms of skilled, semiskilled, and service workers, thus omitting laborers, farm laborers, all other farm-related employees, and homemakers. The sizes of these latter categories have radically declined over the course of the period being considered, and their diminished size becomes an important part of the analysis. Separating them from the rest of the working class helps achieve temporal comparability in the present analysis. (Unfortunately, the ANES has not provided the coded occupational data since 2004.)

In most instances, the direction of year-to-year movement in support is similar across occupational categories. That is, good Democratic years demonstrate an increase in Democratic support among all three categories, and bad Democratic years demonstrate a decrease across all three categories. At the same time, the overall direction of relative support levels within the three occupational categories reverses the ordering of the three groups through time, both in the nation as a

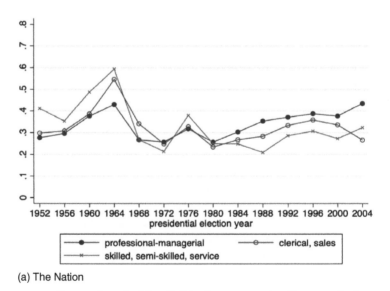

(a) The Nation

FIGURE 7.1. Proportion of white eligible electorate voting Democratic, by presidential election year and occupational class.

(continued)

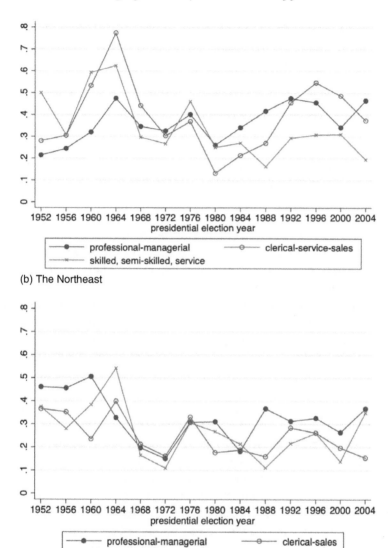

(b) The Northeast

(c) The South

FIGURE 7.1 *(continued)*

whole and in the Northeast. We see a relative increase in professional-managerial support for the Democrats, and a relative decrease in support among the skilled, unskilled, and service group, with the clerical and sales categories typically somewhere in the middle. Indeed, the proportion supporting the Democratic candidates has been higher among professional-managerial respondents than among skilled, semiskilled, and service respondents since 1980.

At the end of the period, we thus see a class inversion in support of the Democrats, where the highest level of support comes from the professional-managerial group, and the lowest level comes from either the clerical and sales category or the working-class category. At the same time, the difference between occupational classes is seldom dramatic. That is, the class basis of the coalition falls short of creating a class-based polarization in Democratic support. The size of the gap between the working class and the professional-managerial categories is relatively constant but reversed in direction between the beginning and the end of the period.

The pattern is similar across the national, northern, and southern samples, but the southern states show a sharper decline in support for Democratic candidates, and professional-managerial respondents are more likely to vote Democratic during both the earlier and later parts of the series. Thus, we see the residue of the old solid Democratic South at the beginning of the period. Virtually all southern whites were likely to vote for the Democrats, and the highest levels of Democratic support occurred among the professional-managerial class.

Figure 7.2 repeats the analysis of Figure 7.1 but employs a measure of Democratic support defined as a proportion of the two-party vote. The two-party vote measure makes the working class appear to be fairly consistently stronger in its support for the Democratic Party. In other words, if we ignore the problem of turnout differentials, the working-class respondents typically show higher levels of support for the Democratic Party. Even here, the level of working-class support declines relative to professional-managerial support across time. Particularly in the Northeast, we see the familiar inversion of support for the Democrats across time. Prior to 1988, the working class typically demonstrates the highest level of support for the Democrats. In 1988 and beyond, working-class support is either less than or indistinguishable from Democratic support among the other two occupational classes.

The South shows a pattern in which all three groups show lower levels of support for the Democratic Party, but the ordering of the occupational categories does not demonstrate any dramatic or consistent

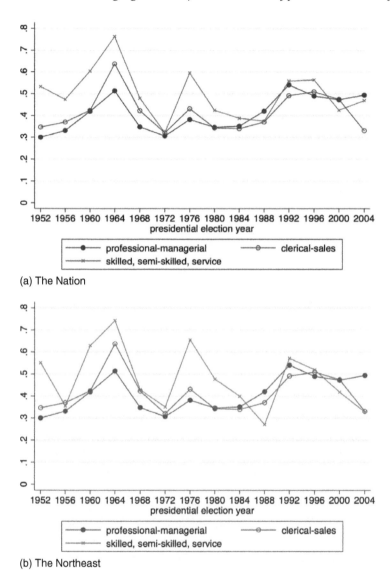

(a) The Nation

(b) The Northeast

FIGURE 7.2. Proportion of white two-party electorate voting Democratic, by occupational class.

(continued)

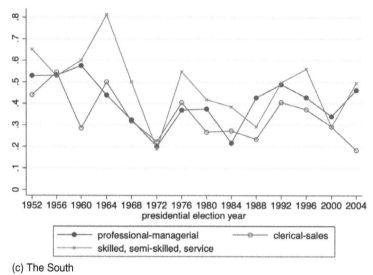

(c) The South

FIGURE 7.2 *(continued)*

change through time. *Indeed, the preferences of southern voters were not structured by class either at the beginning or at the end of the period.* All three groups declined in support for the Democrats, and the differences between the groups (except for 1960, 1964, and 2004) are not pronounced. In short, we see little evidence that the southern white working-class and clerical-sales individuals became more likely than white professional-managerial classes to embrace the Democratic Party (but see Shafer and Johnston 2009).

In summary, these patterns of change in Figures 7.1 and 7.2 show a general weakening of the working-class base for the Democratic Party, while Democratic support among the other two occupational classes has generally increased, *except in the South.* Among southerners, Democratic support among all three occupational groups has generally declined.

The transformation of American party politics is not simply the result of changing support levels within occupational groups, however. Two additional factors have been influential in generating a transformation of the electoral landscape: (1) the success of both the civil rights movement and the Democratic party in mobilizing and incorporating minority voters and (2) fundamental changes in the political economy that have produced a dramatic shift in the composition of the both the labor force and the electorate.

CHANGING LEVELS OF TURNOUT BY RACE AND ETHNICITY

Minority populations realized important advances in the protection of their voting rights due to national civil rights legislation (Kousser 2008), and local Democratic Party organizations have increasingly come to rely on the support of minority populations in local elections. The successes of these local efforts were replicated in a broad range of local elections. African American and Hispanic mayoral candidates have been elected across the country in Los Angeles, San Antonio, Chicago, Philadelphia, and many other cities as well (Browning, Marshall, and Tabb 1986; Sonenshein 1993). Not only has minority electoral success been possible due to the political incorporation of minority groups into local political affairs but minority voters have also become a crucial part of the Democratic Party's national coalition.

Figure 7.3 demonstrates the enhanced role of minority populations in terms of turnout in presidential and congressional elections. These figures are certainly inflated because they rely on self-reports of participation, but the directions of change are clear. At the same time that self-reported turnout among whites has been declining, self-reported turnout among ethnic and racial minorities has been increasing.

First, we see an enormous 1950s gap in reported turnout among whites in comparison to blacks and other racial groups. Overall, the level of white turnout declines over time, and the level of turnout among blacks and other groups increases. Hence, the gap has been greatly reduced by the end of the period. Second, and as Figure 7.4 shows, the result has been a substantial increase in the proportion of the Democratic presidential vote provided by African Americans and other minorities. In short, the partisan impact of the decline in Democratic support shown in Figures 7.1 and 7.2 is partially offset by a corresponding increase in the mobilization and support among minority voters, and the result produces a transformed Democratic Party.

CHANGING POLITICAL DEMOGRAPHY

Dramatic changes have also occurred in the racial, ethnic, and demographic composition of the American population, and these changes are reflected in the weighted ANES survey data. Approximately 90 percent of the sample was white in 1952, with approximately 10 percent African American, and negligible levels of other nonwhite groups. By 2004 the African American population had increased modestly relative to the 1952

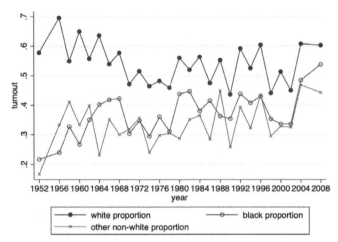

FIGURE 7.3. Turnout among whites, blacks, and other nonwhites in presidential and congressional elections.

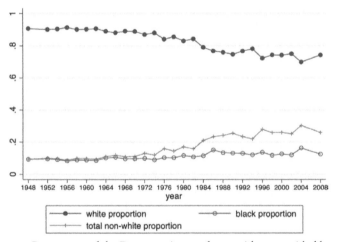

FIGURE 7.4. Percentage of the Democratic vote for president provided by whites, blacks, and nonwhites.

level, but the nonwhite population, which includes African Americans, had increased to more than 20 percent of the population.

At the beginning of the 1950s, approximately 10 percent of the population was nonwhite, and approximately 20 percent of the nonwhite population turned out and voted. Hence, even if the minority population was fully mobilized in support of the Democratic Party, it constituted a relatively small proportion of the Democratic electorate. In contrast, the self-reported turnout of the minority population was approximately 50 percent in 2004, and it constituted more than 20 percent of the population. In short, one dramatic change that occurred in the American electorate during this period was the demographic growth and political mobilization of nonwhite voters in the American electorate.

The occupational structure of the population was also transformed during the fifty-year period we are considering. Figure 7.5 employs US Census data to address the changing class composition, among the entire population (Part A) and among whites alone (Part B), beginning in 1920. The figure shows that the population of skilled and unskilled individuals within the working-class category declined in relative size during the latter part of this period, while two other working-class categories – laborers and agricultural employees – nearly disappeared as significant parts of the national population.

In summary, the process transforming the occupational structure, as well as the demographic decline of the American working class, extends back in time to the early part of the twentieth century. (For a useful comparison to the European version of this process, see

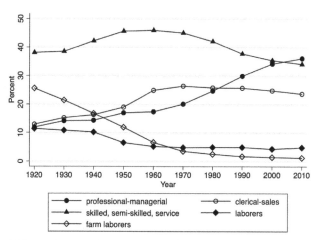

(a) Occupational distribution for the entire US population

FIGURE 7.5. The changing occupational structure from the US Census, 1920–2010. *Source:* Data generated from IPUMS-USA, using the 1950 standardized occupation codes.

(continued)

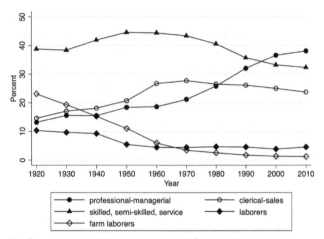

(b) Occupational distribution for white US population

(c) Occupational distribution for white US population with combined
working class

FIGURE 7.5 *(continued)*

Przeworski and Sprague 1986.) Whether looking at the entire workforce (Part A), or just the white workforce (Part B), we see a stark
change in its class composition. Finally, Part C of Figure 7.5 combines
all laborers with skilled, semiskilled, and service workers, illustrating
the demographic decline in the white working classes in a particularly
dramatic fashion. The question that arises is whether these working-
class groups can be understood as sharing common political preferences and interests.

PARTY POLITICS AND STRANGE BEDFELLOWS

An important issue thus relates to the shared political preferences among whites within three occupational classes: (1) skilled, semiskilled, and service; (2) laborers and farmworkers; and (3) professional-managerial. The first group declined in relative size, the second group virtually disappeared as a significant part of the labor force, and the third group increased dramatically. Depending on the patterns of convergence and divergence of group-based preferences among these groups, the implications may or may not be profound.

Table 7.1 shows the results for a series of simple regressions that examine the extent of shared voting preferences among these three groups. The data for the regressions come from Figures 7.1 and 7.2, which show the proportion of respondents within each group who report voting Democratic in the relevant presidential election, both to the base of eligibles and to the base of the two-party vote. In each regression, the vote share among either the professional-managerial respondents or the farm and nonfarm laborers is regressed on the vote share of the working class. Hence, the results provide a measure of shared political preferences among the skilled-unskilled-service group and the other two occupational categories.

The results show a closer correspondence of the skilled-unskilled-service voting preferences with those of the laborers and less correspondence with the professional-managerial class. Hence, not only has the skilled-unskilled-service population declined in relative size but it also lost an important ally with the dramatic decline of the laboring class. Moreover, the divergence in preferences with their new coalition partner – the professional-managerial group – becomes clear. Significant levels of political heterogeneity exist within all these classes, but the political affinity between the two working classes as opposed to the political divergence between the professional-managerial and the skilled-unskilled workers looms as an important distinction.

The divergence between skilled and unskilled workers and the professional-managerial sector looms particularly large in the context of Democratic Party politics. In particular, the professional classes within the industries of law, medicine, and finance claim a disproportionate share of national income and make up a disproportionate share of the top 1 percent relative to other advanced postindustrial nations (Rothwell 2017). Indeed, recent accounts identify these groups as a major factor behind the overall growth in the national income share obtained by

TABLE 7.1. *Shared votes of the skilled and unskilled working class with professional-managerial and farm and nonfarm laborers*

A. Professional-managerial vote for Democratic presidential candidate by the skilled-unskilled vote, as proportions of eligible voters

	Coefficient	Standard Error	t	
Working class	0.2538875	0.1467065	1.73	$R^2 = 0.20$
Constant	0.4935834	0.0996789	4.95	$N = 14$

B. Farm and nonfarm laborer vote for Democratic presidential candidate by skilled-unskilled vote, as proportions of eligible voters

	Coefficient	Standard Error	t	
Working class	0.8960588	0.1398076	6.41	$R^2 = 0.77$
Constant	0.1370927	0.0949915	1.44	$N = 14$

C. Professional-managerial vote for Democratic presidential candidate by skilled-unskilled vote, as proportions of two-party voters

	Coefficient	Standard Error	t	
Working class	0.3460179	0.1789964	1.93	$R^2 = 0.24$
Constant	0.4178314	0.0919873	4.54	$N = 14$

D. Farm and nonfarm laborer vote for Democratic presidential candidate by skilled-unskilled vote, as proportions of two-party voters

	Coefficient	Standard Error	t	
Working class	0.8800521	0.1715144	5.13	$R^2 = 0.69$
Constant	0.1576787	0.0881423	1.79	$N = 14$

the most affluent 1 percent – a growth primarily fueled by salaries rather than dividends.

Many within the professional classes continue to support the Republican Party, but a major and increasing share has migrated to the Democrats. The white, nativist, and neopopulist impulses that have emerged within the contemporary Republican Party fail to attract many within these professional classes, at the same time that their own interests are not easily reconciled with the more traditional, multiracial social welfare instincts of the Democratic Party. Hence, we see politicians like the current Democratic Senate Minority Leader caught between a rock and a hard place – attempting to fulfill the social welfare mandate of a party that has lost a major part of its white populist base. In short, the Republicans' white populist rebellion has, in fact, turned populism upside down.

ROCKS, HARD PLACES, AND THE POLITICAL ROLE OF LABOR UNIONS

While the working class has declined as a proportion of the American population, labor unions – the champions of working-class interests – have been in a free fall. Part A of Figure 7.6 shows the rapid growth of unions that began in the late 1930s as a consequence of the Fair Labor Standards Act and other sympathetic legislative and administrative treatment during the New Deal. Membership growth continued at a slower rate in the 1950s, peaked in the late 1970s, and has stayed relatively stable with a modest downward trend since that time.

During this post–World War II period of slow growth in membership followed by a slow decline, the American workforce has grown at a rapid rate. Thus, Part B of Figure 7.6, which shows the percent of employed workers who are unionized, presents a far different reality. The *percent* of employed workers who are unionized reached its peak in the 1950s and then declined to levels not seen since the 1930s. As a percentage of the workforce, labor union membership is back where it began in the period prior to the 1935 adoption of the Fair Labor Standards Act. Moreover, Parts C and D of Figure 7.6 show that the decline in union membership is not restricted to particular industries but is widespread across occupational groups.

In short, labor union membership has lost ground even more rapidly than the working-class population. More importantly, at the same time that the group has lost political influence due to its declining size, its primary organizational champion has declined as well. And thus, a primary mainstay within the organizational life of the Democratic Party is occupying a diminished role not only in the economy but in the political system as well.

IMPLICATIONS FOR THE DEMOCRATIC COALITION

Most of this discussion, as well as most discussions of electoral politics, tends to focus on the rate at which different groups vote for a particular party. *Equally important for purposes of party politics and governance is the proportion of a party's coalition that is composed of various groups.* A primary survival instinct of political

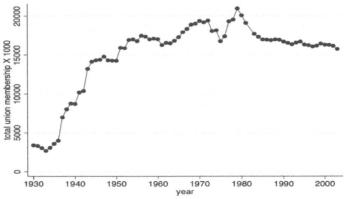

(a) Total union membership

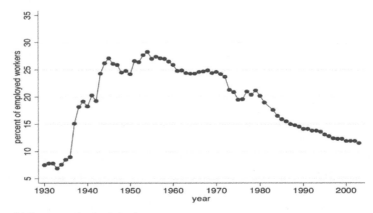

(b) Percent unionized, workers

FIGURE 7.6. Union membership in the United States. (*Source:* Gerald Mayer. "Union Membership Trends in the United States." Congressional Resource Service. http://digitalcommons.ilr.cornell.edu. (Data are missing for 1982.)

(continued)

parties and candidates is to maintain their political coalitions, and hence, they will act in ways that represent their crucial constituencies. Of course, different politicians within the same party depend on different constituencies to various degrees. At the same time, we can still think of the strength and vitality of various party constituencies being reflected by their proportional representation among all the party supporters. That is, the proportional size of a group within the party's coalition is reflective of its overall strength and influence within the party.

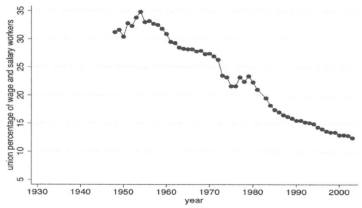

(c) Percent unionized, wage and salary workers

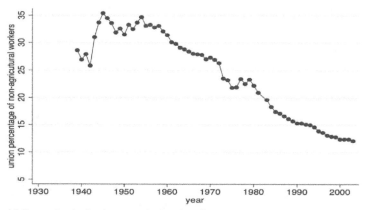

(d) Percent unionized, non-agricultural workers

FIGURE 7.6 *(continued)*

Part A of Figure 7.7 shows the group proportions of the national Democratic vote for president provided by various key constituencies: white professional-managerial, white clerical-sales, white working class, African American, and other nonwhites. Until the late 1960s, the white working class was the undisputed heavyweight within the national Democratic coalition. Indeed, nearly half of the Democratic electoral coalition was provided by the white working class in 1960. In 2004, the African American and white professional-managerial populations each contributed somewhat less than 30 percent of the Democratic Party's support, and the white working class provided slightly less than 20 percent. In short, the party has been transformed from a party dominated by the white working class to a party with significant support coming from a

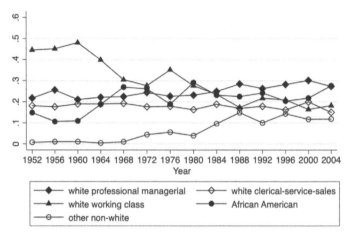

(a) Group proportions of national Democratic vote for president

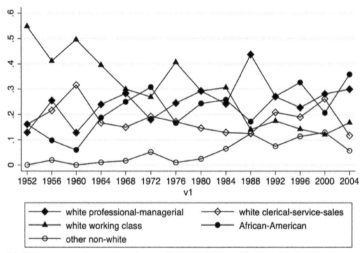

(b) Group proportions of northeast Democratic presidential vote

FIGURE 7.7. Class and racial composition of the Democratic coalition.

(continued)

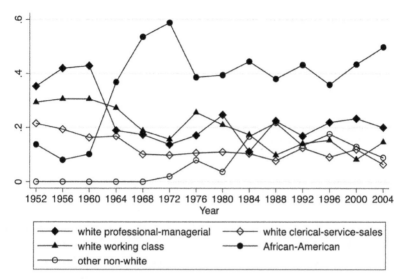

(c) Group proportions of southern Democratic presidential vote

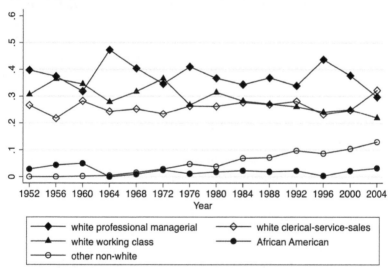

(d) Group proportions of the national Republican vote

FIGURE 7.7 *(continued)*

range of groups, and the relative role of the white working class is dramatically diminished.

The most important thing to note is that the role of the white working class has diminished not simply as a consequence of low levels of support among white workers. Rather, the role of the white working class is a function of its own demographic decline as well as both the political mobilization of other racial and ethnic minorities and the continuing conversion of the professional-managerial ranks to the Democratic Party.

The pattern of support shown in Part A of Figure 7.7 changes quite dramatically across different regions of the country. In Part B of Figure 7.7, we see the structure of the Democratic Party coalition in the Northeast for the same period. The reliance on the white working class is even more pronounced in the early 1950s, and yet its decline is even more dramatic. In 1952 it accounted for more than 50 percent of Democratic presidential votes, and by 2004 it provided less than 20 percent. In contrast, the white professional-managerial voters provided slightly more than 10 percent of the support in 1952, but 30 percent in 2004. African Americans and other nonwhites accounted for less than 20 percent of party votes in 1952, but more than 40 percent in 2004.

The most dramatic pattern of change occurs in the southern pattern of support for the Democrats shown in Part C of Figure 7.7. From 1952 to 1960, prior to the 1964 Civil Rights Act and the 1965 Voting Rights Act, less than 20 percent of Democratic support came from African Americans. In 1972, they provided nearly 60 percent of the Democratic presidential vote in the South. In contrast, the white supporters of the party declined from more than 80 percent in 1952 to less than 50 percent in 2004. And as we have seen earlier, Democrats have not won a majority of the white vote in a presidential vote since 1964.

Finally, for comparison, Part D of Figure 7.7 presents the group proportions of the national Republican vote. For the entirety of the period, whites make up the vast majority of Republican voters. There was a slight uptick of nonwhite voters in 2000 and 2004. But even here the Republican coalition remains mostly white, providing 85 percent of Republican votes in 2004. The professional-managerial class constituted the largest group for most of this period although their presence dipped in the 2004 election. White working-class voters also became slightly less pronounced in the Republican coalition, but compared to the Democrats, the Republicans became more dependent on white working class and white clerical-service-sales support.

WHAT HAVE WE LEARNED?

The analyses of this chapter carry several important implications based on the post–World War II transformations of American politics and the party coalitions. First, among whites in the early 1950s, professional-managerial voters were least likely to vote Democratic, but by 2004 they were the most likely, not only in the Northeast but in the nation as a whole. This is particularly important because the white electorate was predominantly working class until the early 1990s, when the professional-managerial classes overtook it.

These patterns reflect larger trends in the national economy in which the supply of working-class jobs was proportionately declining at the same time as the supply of professional-managerial jobs was growing rapidly. Moreover, the contemporary remnant of the working-class Democratic electorate is almost entirely composed of clerical, service, and sales workers. Skilled and unskilled labor has precipitously declined as a percentage of the workforce, and hence, as a percentage of the Democratic electorate.

Second, at the same time that turnout among white voters was in decline, turnout was rapidly increasing among African Americans and other racial-ethnic groups. Hence, the nonwhite percentage of the total national Democratic vote for president increased from 10 percent to nearly 25 percent. As the party of civil rights, Democrats became increasingly reliant on the votes of nonwhites. Hence, the Democratic Party has become increasingly reliant on the votes of well-educated whites and racial-ethnic minorities, and the white working class no longer occupies center stage within the Democratic coalition.

The problem is that it has been all too tempting for Democratic politicians to ignore the problems of class that extend across racial and ethnic divides. Working-class Americans of all races and ethnicities share common problems and challenges, and a successful Democratic Party needs to create a combined appeal based on class-based challenges as well as race-based challenges. Creating a coalition that combines white professional-managerial voters with the white working-class voters and minority voters may appear to be a difficult task, but such a feat is not unprecedented, and it holds the key to the Democratic Party's future.

The alternative would appear to be the continuing loss of working-class influence within the party, as well as a decline of support for the party within the working class, thereby creating continuing opportunities for regressive populists. Defining the working class in terms of income, Bartels (2006) and Stonecash (2000) argue that support for the

Democrats among the white working class has not declined. Defining the working class in terms of educational level, Abramowitz and Teixeira (2009) argue that the support for the Democratic Party has declined within a working class that is *itself* in proportional decline within the American population. Our own results, based on occupational class, coincide with their observations. The consequences have been particularly profound in the South, where the Democratic Party has become dramatically dependent on support among African American voters.

Finally, the decline of unions and union membership has been an important part of the Democratic Party's problem. Once again, however, we should not ignore the larger context of the dramatic economic transformation and its implications for the American workforce. Modernization of production coupled with international trade and inexpensive labor has minimized the opportunities for blue-collar workers – skilled or unskilled. In a very real sense, the modernization of the workforce combined with the mobilization of racial and ethnic minorities and the growth of the educated professional classes has driven a stake into the heart of the traditional New Deal coalition, as well as dramatically undermining the American labor movement.

The political implications are profound, creating important challenges for both parties as well as for the future of democratic politics in the United States. Fewer working-class individuals, both white and nonwhite, are struggling to secure diminishing opportunities for working-class employment. Due to the loss of manufacturing jobs and the concomitant decline in labor unions, the possibilities for an affluent working-class lifestyle have been severely diminished. Hence, it is not surprising that shrinking economic opportunity has made it difficult for working-class whites and nonwhites to collaborate in the same political coalition, particularly when regressive populists stoke the fires of racial competition.

CONCLUSION: UNDERSTANDING THE POLITICAL IMPLICATIONS

We have documented several important political and demographic changes within the electorate. First, our argument is that the white working class has become a problematic constituency for the Democratic Party, whose support for the party has declined over the long haul. Certainly, Donald Trump's candidacy has shown that the party has difficulty maintaining white working-class support. Even more fundamentally, however, the white working class demonstrates a dramatic demographic decline as a percentage of the population, and hence, as a group to be reckoned with in Democratic Party politics. While it provided a solid base for the New Deal Democratic Party, it has declined to the status of, at best, a minority partner in the modern party.

Second, the white professional-managerial class has undergone its own great migration out of the Republican Party and toward the Democrats. The migration is less than complete, but members of this class now constitute, along with African Americans, one of the two main constituencies within the Democratic Party's electoral coalition. This explains a number of contemporary phenomena, including why the Democrats are attracted to support for economic issues like free trade and other similar political-economic issues, thereby putting themselves at cross purposes with many members of the working-class electorate regarding a wide range of other economic issues. It also explains why more traditional Republicans are having difficulty with their party's desertion of formerly core principles, such as free trade (Flake 2017).

Why have so many of the professional-managerial class migrated to the Democrats? Certainly many within the class continue to be attracted to the free enterprise model supported by mainline Republican politicians and have stayed within Republican ranks, but others with similar economic and social views have settled in the Democratic Party. This analysis suggests, however, that the professional-managerial class is composed of several distinctive political orientations. One reason for the professional-managerial migration to the Democrats is undoubtedly due to the white populist rebellion that found a home in the Republican Party with Barry Goldwater's candidacy in 1964 and remains an important source of Republican support in 2016. Many within the professional-managerial class are undoubtedly ill at ease with those elements of the Republican Party and hence have found the Democrats to be the preferred alternative. Moreover, in the context of the modern capitalist economy, many might believe that contemporary Democrats are better economic managers. And indeed, Democrats generate sufficient support from Wall Street to sustain such a belief.

Not only has the working class declined as a proportion of the population and as a base of support for the Democratic Party, but so also has trade unionism. With the exception of public employee unions, most major American unions are in retreat along a number of fronts, and this too carries particularly important implications for the Democrats. These unions had become a major voice for a wide range of liberal political causes, and the loss of their support benefits some interests and furthers others, both within and beyond the Democratic Party.

All this produces major implications for public policy in the United States. In the context of a declining working-class and neutralized unions, a Democratic Party that depends on the support of the upper-middle class will ultimately see the political and economic virtues of supporting policies such as free trade. Hence, a Republican populist candidate like Donald Trump is quite willing to profess his love for the "poorly educated," while Senator Charles Schumer, the influential Democratic senator from New York, is willing to tell the Washington Press Club that he thinks the Democratic Party "blew it" in providing health insurance for the uninsured because it "made no political sense."

In short, few contemporary Democrats would be willing to employ the rhetoric of Roosevelt's 1936 Madison Square Garden that we quoted earlier. Roosevelt's speech makes the rhetoric of Bernie Sanders look tame by comparison, and many Democratic voters would undoubtedly reject any contemporary Democratic candidate using such class-based strident language. Even those in agreement might view the candidate as being unelectable, and they might be correct.

The Democratic Party is no longer primarily dependent on working-class votes. This fact helps explain both (1) why populism has been turned on its head politically and (2) how Donald Trump, a Republican billionaire, is able to construct a populist message that appeals successfully to those who are, in his words, "poorly educated." Perhaps more remarkably, it helps explain why the current Democratic Minority Leader in the Senate, who has led the fight to maintain the Affordable Care Act (ACA), is the same individual who, in 2014, declared that the ACA was a mistaken effort aimed at people who did not vote at sufficient levels to make the effort politically worthwhile. Hence, in Chapter 8 we consider the implications for the 2016 presidential election. In particular, we consider the construction of the party coalitions and the sources of their votes relative to occupational classes and racial-ethnic groups.

APPENDIX 7.A

EDUCATIONAL ATTAINMENT AND SUPPORT FOR THE PARTIES

Chapter 7 employs occupational categories as the basis for examining voting support across economic classes during the past half-century. Unfortunately, data on occupations are unavailable in the ANES cumulative file after 2004. To overcome this problem, we augment the analysis by examining voting support across categories of educational attainment from 1952 to 2016. Abramowitz and Teixeira (2009) have argued that educational attainment – and in particular, the completion of a college degree – closely tracks occupational categories and economic class. For instance, today most managerial and professional occupations require, at minimum, a BA degree.

Figure 7.A1 displays the rates of support for Democratic presidential candidates among (white) college-educated voters and (white) non-college-educated voters. Support for the Democrats among white college-educated voters has increased in recent elections. At the same time, support for the Democrats among white noncollege graduates has decreased. In 1952 24.5 percent of white college graduates voted Democratic. By 2016, 55.2 percent of white college-educated voters supported the Democratic candidate. By contrast, only 34.1 percent of white noncollege voters chose Clinton in 2016, while the

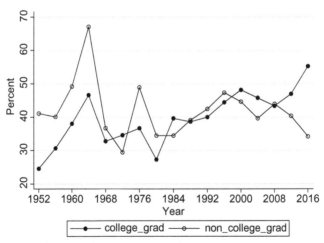

FIGURE 7.A1. Educational attainment and Democratic Party support among (white) voters, 1952–2016.

Republican Party is becoming more reliant on non-college-educated voters. Nowhere was this more evident than in the 2016 election. As Donald Trump declared during the 2016 Republican primaries, and quoted at the beginning of this chapter, "We won with the poorly educated. I love the poorly educated." There was a good reason behind his declaration. In 2016, 65.9 percent of white noncollege voters supported Trump. As these data show, the analysis of occupational class and populist politics is reinforced by an analysis of education.

8

Dueling Populists and the Political Ecology of 2016

The 2016 presidential election demonstrated a dramatic resurgence of populism in American politics, in which the three most successful candidates – Trump, Clinton, and Sanders – advanced their own distinctive populist brands. Trump's promise to "make America great again" involved a direct appeal to a socially and economically struggling white working class. Clinton's campaign focused attention on the concerns of women, minorities, and the disadvantaged, at the same time that she cultivated support on Wall Street. As a democratic socialist, Sanders challenged Clinton's campaign for the Democratic nomination from the left, advocating extended social welfare benefits and free higher education.

These three candidates and their campaigns reflected the variegated history of populist appeals in American politics. Trump's campaign reflected a regressive, divisive brand of populism with a long history in American politics that has been particularly vibrant in the American South. Sanders represented the democratic socialist tradition that has historically experienced the most difficulty in gaining a resilient base of support in American politics. And Hillary Clinton represented a moderate brand of American populism that attempts to embrace the values of political and social equality while maintaining the support of American business.

In an election year of dueling populists, it is perhaps ironic that a Republican populist was the ultimate Electoral College victor, even though he was an outsider within the Republican Party establishment. At the same time, the 2016 election illustrates the resilience of the conservative, regressive form of populism in American politics, as well as the continuing challenges to progressive populist traditions. This chapter addresses the historic roots of the various populist appeals as well as connects them to contemporary American politics.

THE AMERICAN POPULIST TRADITION

Populist politicians have a long and frequently controversial history in American politics. The populist brand is often associated with rabble-rousing political figures, typically but not always located in southern states, who have mobilized individuals to anger, political activism, anger, ethnic and racial rivalry, and sometimes violent responses to perceived injustices. Huey Long, Tom Watson, and Theodore Bilbo stand out as examples of populist politicians in the history of American politics for their fiery rhetoric and incendiary messages regarding the exploitation of the common citizen by rapacious elites, as well as by cultural outsiders or racial-ethnic minorities.

Mississippi's Bilbo was an unscrupulous and virulent racist who engaged in rabble-rousing, directed not only at offending elites but also at innocent bystanders, in this case, African Americans (Key 1949). Georgia's Watson (Woodward 1938) started out as an anti-elite leader of the Populist Party who attempted to combine whites and blacks in a common movement, but he ultimately deteriorated into a nativist advocate of disadvantaged whites at the expense of blacks, Catholics, and Jews. Long won support among both whites and blacks for his populist and frequently antidemocratic responses to the problems of poverty and corporate influence in pre–World War II Louisiana. Indeed, Long was a particularly controversial figure, in life as well as in death. Various accounts of his demise have flourished, but T. Harry Williams, his primary biographer, documents an assassin motivated by fear and antipathy anchored in the privileges of race and class in Louisiana politics (Williams 1970: 866–872).[1]

---

[1] Controversy and conflicting accounts continue to surround the account of Long's assassination, leading to an exhumation and autopsy of Dr. Carl Weiss, the purported assassin, more than sixty-five years after his death (*New York Times*, 1991). The results of the autopsy were inconclusive, however, and an abundant list of Long's enemies have been offered up as potential candidates. In the words of journalist Betty Carter, the wife of crusading anti-Long journalist Hodding Carter, regarding the identity of Long's assassin, "You didn't know who it was. It could have been anybody" (Burns 1986). The controversy surrounding Long is reinforced by Key's (1949) seminal account of southern politics.

In contrast to Donald Trump, and regardless of all of Long's short-comings, the Long faction was a populist movement that actually pursued tangible material benefits for the disadvantaged classes (Williams 1970; Liebling 1978). More importantly, the administrations of Franklin Roosevelt's New Deal and Lyndon Johnson's Great Society continue to stand out as the exemplars of the American populist impulse being translated into policies that produced genuine social and economic benefits for disadvantaged Americans.

The continuing problem, for both the practice and analysis of politics, is that populists and populism come in a variety of forms communicating a range of political messages. Indeed, their only point of commonality is that they all attempt to mobilize a socially and economically disadvantaged portion of the electorate. As we have noted in Chapter 3, Franklin Roosevelt used strong populist language in addressing the "old enemies of peace – business and financial monopoly, speculation, reckless banking, class antagonism, sectionalism, war profiteering." He employed the strong words of a committed populist, and many have considered him to be both a scoundrel and a "traitor to his class" (Brand 2008). At the same time, no credible accounting of Roosevelt's populist presidency would put him in the same league with Theodore Bilbo. Populism is not, in short, a vulgarity unless it has become politically unacceptable and unconscionable for politicians to mobilize disadvantaged citizens for the advancement of their shared interests. Still, as Bernie Sanders has demonstrated, the effort to legitimate "democratic socialism" is an uphill struggle, as is the resurrection of liberal populism.

The fact remains that neither populism nor democratic socialism can be divorced from the history or the conceptual apparatus of American politics, and as the 2016 campaign demonstrated, populism is the sole domain of neither Democrats nor Republicans (Edsall 2017). Both the Democratic and Republican candidates constructed their own version of a populist appeal to the American electorate during the 2016 presidential election. This chapter addresses the distinctions among populist appeals, as well as the implications both for the shape of resulting coalitions and electoral politics going forward.

POPULISTS, MARKETS, AND THE DEMOCRATIC BALANCE

American electoral politics has traditionally been motivated by some version of the trade-off between equality and efficiency articulated by Arthur Okun (1975) nearly a half-century ago (also see Stiglitz 2012).

Most typically the Republican Party has argued that economic efficiency requires fiscal and monetary policies aimed at increasing productivity, thus creating the famed rising tide of prosperity. In contrast, the Democratic Party has typically taken a position emphasizing equality and a level playing field – taxing and spending policies aimed at creating economic and social welfare benefits for economically disadvantaged citizens.

Significant partisan deviations from these positions have occurred on a recurrent basis. Lyndon Johnson famously endorsed the "rising tide of prosperity that lifts all ships" in his 1964 message to Congress, and Republican members of Congress cautiously avoid taking responsibility for the loss of social welfare benefits. More generally, business-friendly Democrats and working-class-friendly Republicans have typically (but neither recently nor always) converged toward the median voter in their efforts at balancing taxing, spending, and the creation of social welfare benefits. As Okun made clear, a strong case can be made for *both* efficiency *and* equality in sustaining economic growth within the context of a democratic political system.

In this context, Hillary Clinton fit the mold of a business-friendly Democrat in her 2016 presidential election. While she reached out to citizens of modest means in a number of ways and across a range of venues, she also pursued a strategy aimed at raising campaign funds among technology executives and the titans of Wall Street, as well as cultivating support among small-business entrepreneurs. She embraced a number of Wall Street–favored policies, as well as programmatic efforts on behalf of the working class that tended to focus on retraining programs that would make individuals more competitive in a rapidly changing job market. She had been an earlier supporter of the Trans-Pacific Partnership (TPP) trade deal as a secretary of state in the Obama administration but came out against it as a presidential candidate. Many Democratic voters, not limited to supporters of Bernie Sanders, would argue that she went too far in efforts aimed at cultivating Wall Street support. At the same time, she was also attentive to traditional Democratic constituencies, with a particular focus on working people, small-business entrepreneurs, women, poor people, and ethnic and racial minorities.

In contrast, Donald Trump constructed an appeal that was in many ways divorced from Republican orthodoxy. He opposed international trade deals, including the TPP and the North American Free Trade Agreement (NAFTA), and he blamed them for sending American jobs overseas. He similarly berated American companies for moving their factories beyond

American borders. And he blamed American immigration policies for both taking jobs away from Americans and creating a range of social problems, including crime and overburdened social services. These positions were sufficiently divergent from traditional Republican themes to alarm a range of traditional Republican constituencies.

At the same time, Trump's strategy produced problems for his Democratic opponents. Indeed, Trump successfully outflanked Clinton on a range of different issues in an effort to neutralize the basis of her appeal. Given her track record on Wall Street and as a fundraiser for the Clinton Foundation, she was particularly vulnerable to Trump's own populist strategy.

Hence, both candidates made efforts to embrace the aspirations of working- and middle-class Americans. Both candidates constructed their own populist appeals, even though their respective appeals diverged from each other in dramatic (if sometimes unappreciated) ways. Indeed, the election can be seen as a battle between dueling populists – candidates who made strong claims to loyalties of voters at the lower end of the income distribution with divergent visions of the country, its problems, and its future (Hout 2008). In this context, we address a series of questions.

How should we understand the divergent forms of populism advocated by the candidates? How important was the race, class, and ethnic background of voters relative to each of the candidate's appeals? How important were traditional party loyalties for candidate choice? What are the implications for the future of partisan politics in American elections? How important was social welfare policy, and in particular, the Affordable Care Act (ACA), to Trump's ultimately victorious populist message to the American voters? Finally, what role did racial hostility play in Trump's success? We address these questions based on data taken from the 2016 Cooperative Congressional Election Study (CCES), an online nationally stratified sample survey conducted by YouGov, including both preelection and postelection interviews with more than 50,000 respondents.

GETTING A GRIP ON DUELING POPULISTS
IN AMERICAN POLITICS

This chapter is based on the argument that populism is not necessarily a bad word, and that the populist instinct comes in a variety of shapes and sizes bearing little resemblance to one another. As we have seen, the list of populists in American political history ranges from the villainous Mississippi race-baiter Theodore Bilbo to the legendary Franklin Roosevelt who mobilized Americans in the fight against fascism as well as in support of economic reform, labor legislation, and social welfare measures aimed at ameliorating the worst financial catastrophe in American history.

The important issues relate to the fundamental distinction between what can be called progressive and regressive forms of populism. The goal of a progressive populism is to further the freedom and well-being of economically disadvantaged citizens at the lower end of the economic spectrum, regardless of race or ethnicity. And thus, it is progressive in the sense of bringing people with shared interests together in the same political movement, thereby furthering some form of a democratic consensus. Reasonable individuals might certainly disagree regarding the wisdom of such action within the context of various economic circumstances. Returning to Okun's analysis, a populist movement might be socially and politically beneficial if it restored the balance between equality and efficiency in a way that strengthened the underlying political economy. Alternatively, a populist movement might be ruinous if it successfully pursued goals that instead undermined economic efficiency in a way that ultimately made all interests suffer.

Hence, whether a progressive populist party, candidate, or cause is worthy of support is contingent on the implications it carries in the political-economic context of a particular time and place. Within the context of the currently high and increasing levels of income equality in the United States (Bartels 2008; Bonica et al. 2013; Piketty 2014; Piketty and Saez 2003), the case for a populist movement would seem straightforward. At the same time, reasonable citizens – even reasonable populists – might very well disagree regarding appropriate courses of action depending on current economic circumstances.

In contrast, regressive populist movements have been uniformly on the wrong side of democratic norms as well as the wrong side of history. Unlike a progressive populist impulse aimed at furthering social welfare and economic well-being among the disadvantaged, regressive populist movements employ ethnic and racial hostilities to divide, manipulate, and conquer the rank and file of disadvantaged citizens who might be mobilized by a populist appeal. Rather than an attempt to bring voters together based on shared interests, it attempts to fracture a political movement using wedge issues such as race, ethnicity, and religious background.

Mississippi's Bilbo remains the paradigmatic example of the shameless populist manipulator, as he instigated and accelerated racial conflict in his effort to wrestle political control in Depression-era Mississippi (Key 1949). He has, however, bequeathed his skill set to a new generation of political actors, and the spirit of Bilbo is very much alive and thriving in contemporary American politics.

DONALD TRUMP AND REGRESSIVE POPULISM

Donald Trump made little effort at winning significant support among racial and ethnic minorities. His appeal to African Americans on August 18, 2016, was, quite literally, "[W]hat do you have to lose?" And his position regarding Latino Americans' immigration, as well as his stance regarding young people covered by Deferred Action for Childhood Arrivals (DACA), served to alienate potential Latino Americans' support. Although he managed to win broader support among African Americans and Latino Americans than Mitt Romney, who had promised to end the DACA program in his own 2012 run for the presidency, NBC exit polls suggest that he won only 8 percent of the African American vote and 29 percent of the Latino American vote.

In contrast, Trump did extremely well among some important groups of white citizens. In spite of the "Access Hollywood" tape revealing Trump's misogynous attitudes, the NBC exit polls show that he won 53 percent of the vote among white women to 43 percent for Clinton, as well as 63 percent of the vote among white men to 31 percent for Clinton. While his positions on immigration and the needs of African Americans did little to attract minority support, he was the runaway favorite among white voters. Indeed, a key to Trump's Electoral College victory was his ability to generate enthusiastic white support in the upper Midwest swing states that were crucial to Clinton's electoral prospects.

Trump's populist appeal can be understood quite well in the context of Bilbo's efforts to stoke the flames of racial and ethnic animosity. His savvy overtures to racial animosity and fear have been recurrent and deft, and his candidacy and popularity have benefitted from a long list of racially provocative statements and events, before, during, and subsequent to the election (Desjardins 2018). At the same time, Trump constructed a record of at least semiplausible deniability that made it possible for those charitably inclined to dismiss charges of racial or ethnic bias in order to maintain the support of voters who might object to his racially charged claims and messages. His mixed bag of racial cues and messages has even included apologies for earlier statements, before continuing on with a stream of similar messages and actions. He thus makes it possible for white voters to infer antiminority positions without committing to specifics, while he preserves deniability.

One of the central actions of his presidential campaign and presidency has been his opposition to the ACA. By campaigning against the signal event of the Obama presidency, he was able to continue the crusade that he began with his evidence-free denial of Obama's citizenship. Both issues, the citizenship claim and opposition to the ACA, carry a renunciation of all things connected to the Obama presidency. And for many voters, this renunciation comes deeply embedded in racial hostility, as well as stimulating a renewal of that animus.

CHANGING TIMES AND THE DEMOCRATIC PARTY'S POPULIST APPEAL

The Democratic Party of Franklin Roosevelt successfully mobilized urban, ethnic, working-class voters during the Great Depression of the 1930s, and it defined the party's modern populist appeal during this period (Katznelson 2013; also see McPherson 1982, 1992). During the darkest days of the Great Depression, it passed the Social Security Act (1935) giving rise to the foundation of the American social welfare state, as well as the National Labor Relations Act (1935) and the Fair Labor Standards Act (1938), which served as the foundation for the American labor movement. During the same period, the Rural Electrification Act (1936) brought electricity to rural areas across the country. These measures, along with the Glass-Steagall Act (1933), which regulated the banking industry, and the Agricultural Adjustment Act (1933), which stabilized agricultural prices, solidified the populist appeal of the Democratic Party and set the stage for Democratic dominance of national government for years to come.

A primary problem of the modern Democratic Party is that demographic and economic transformations have overtaken the groups upon which the earlier period of Democratic ascendancy was based. First, the occupational composition of the American population has been radically transformed. Agricultural modernization created surplus labor throughout the southern and midwestern farming belts. As a consequence, African Americans began to move from the South toward the industrial North and West. Similarly, white farmers in the Midwest began to move off their farms toward urban employment as well.

Second, technology, modernization, and international trade reduced the need for American laborers on factory assembly lines and elsewhere, thus undermining the unionization movement. As we saw in Chapter 7, the percentage of the labor force represented by unions reached its peak in the 1950s and began a sharp and dramatic decline thereafter. Indeed, the contemporary percentage of workers who are unionized is quite close to the level prior to the 1935 National Labor Relations Act.

Hence, the populist appeal of the Democratic Party, as well as the labor union vehicle for that appeal, has been in a long-term historical decline. Support for Roosevelt's party was based on small-scale farmers and unionized manual laborers, but these populations have been proportionally eclipsed as clerical and service occupations' gain in ascendancy, along with a burgeoning professional-managerial population (Rothwell 2017). Moreover, racial heterogeneity among working-class and clerical-service-sales groups has made it more difficult for Democrats to fashion a unifying populist appeal. As a consequence, the working classes no longer provide fertile grounds for the Democrats' populist appeal, and support for the party increasingly comes to reflect the transformed economy.

The two dominant sources of support for the Democratic Party by the turn of the century came from the white professional-managerial class and a diverse range of racial and ethnic groups (Schickler 2016). The white working-class and white clerical-service-sales occupational groups, in contrast, account for significantly smaller elements within the contemporary Democratic coalition, while they continue to be crucial to the party's future success. The Democratic Party's problem is that unifying these multiracial and multiethnic groups has been a formidable task. It is not simply that the Democrats' populist appeal is adrift, but rather that the traditional target of that appeal – the white working class – is no longer the dominant part of the coalition that existed as recently as the early 1960s. Indeed, the party relies on a group – the white professional-managerial population – that is not a primary target for a populist appeal. Hence, the party confronts the problematic task of constructing a multiracial, multiethnic populist appeal when one major portion of its coalition is not naturally attracted by a populist agenda.

None of this is meant to suggest that the electorate is awash in affluence. To the contrary, large parts of the former occupational structure have disappeared; a range of well-paid, lower-skilled employment opportunities have correspondingly been diminished; and national income has become increasingly concentrated within the wealthiest sectors of American society (Bartels 2008; Piketty 2014; Piketty and Saez 2003). These changes set the stage for decreased opportunities and higher levels of working-class disillusionment across racial groups. Indeed, the success of Bernie Sanders' own version of the populist appeal is evidence that the populist opportunity continues to exist for the Democratic Party.

In circumstances such as these, the failure of a progressive populist appeal carries troubling consequences. Using American political history as a guide, it perhaps comes as no surprise that racial tensions have risen, and with that rise comes the opportunity for regressive populism – a populism that stokes the fires of racial conflict and hostility (Hadley 1985; Huckfeldt and Kohfeld 1989). In this context, we turn to an analysis of the resulting implications for the 2016 presidential election.

UPSIDE-DOWN POPULISM IN THE 2016 ELECTION

Donald Trump won the battle of the dueling populists in the 2016 presidential election based on a coalition quite similar to the coalitions that have propelled other Republican presidential candidates to victory since 1964. The 1964 election was the last time that a Democratic Party's presidential candidate was able to achieve majority support among white voters. As Part A of Table 8.1 shows, Donald Trump received 56.4% of the white vote, but only 6% of the African American vote, 24% of the Latino American vote, and 26% of the Asian American vote – results that only slightly diverge from the results from the NBC exit polls cited earlier due to survey methods and measurement error. While these vote shares managed to secure a majority vote in the Electoral College, they failed to produce a popular vote majority.

Hence, the racial distribution of the vote does not appear dissimilar to other elections since 1964, with Democrats receiving widespread support among whites that falls short of a majority, but much stronger support among racial and ethnic majorities. That pattern of support has been sufficient to generate Democratic victories for Carter in 1976, Clinton in 1992 and 1996, and Obama in 2008 and 2012. Indeed, given the great variation in the types of candidates and campaigns, the stability of the underlying party coalitions has been quite striking, and the Donald Trump's election was clearly an extension of these earlier coalition patterns.

Part B of Table 8.1 shows that the vote was highly structured by party. Both candidates obtained something approaching unanimous support among their respective copartisans. This is particularly striking given the huge divide within the Republican electorate during the primary season, as well as the contemporaneous reports and evidence that many Republicans were disquieted by the Trump candidacy. In spite

TABLE 8.1. *Two-party vote for Trump and Clinton by race, party, born-again identification, economic pessimism, and support for the repeal of the Affordable Care Act*

A.

	White	Black	Latino American	Asian	Other	Total	
Trump	56.4%	6.3%	24.3%	26.0%	52.4%	46.5%	N = 38,959
Clinton	43.6%	93.7%	75.7%	74.0%	47.6%	53.5%	
Sample%	72%	12%	7%	4%	4%		

B.

	Democrat	Republican	Independent	Other	Not sure	Total	
Trump	5.7%	93.9%	56.1%	66.9%	53.4%	46.5%	N = 38,951
Clinton	94.3%	6.1%	43.9%	33.1%	46.6%	53.5%	
Sample%	35%	26%	31%	1%	7%		

C.

	Identifies as *born again*	Does not identify *as born again*	Total	
Trump	60.9%	39.2%	46.5%	N = 38,942
Clinton	39.1%	60.8%	53.5%	
Sample%	32%	68%		

D.

	Most economically *optimistic*						Most economically *pessimistic*					
Trump	18%	6%	7%	13%	30%	47%	67%	84%	89%	91%	90%	N = 38,786
Clinton	82%	94%	93%	87%	70%	53%	33%	16%	11%	9%	10%	
Sample%	1%	3%	9%	11%	14%	18%	14%	8%	5%	2%	2%	

E.

	Support repeal of Affordable Care Act?		
	No	Yes	
Trump	10%	76%	N = 38,896
Clinton	90%	24%	
Sample%	46%	54%	

Note: All results in this and the following tables are post-weighted to recover a representative sample.

of intraparty soul-searching, these data suggest that neither candidate suffered from serious defections, regardless of the bizarre events surrounding the Trump campaign, Hillary Clinton's lack of widespread popularity, and the insurgent candidacy of Bernie Sanders. And as Part C of Table 8.1 shows, the "Access Hollywood" tape and other salacious reports were insufficient for Donald Trump to lose majority support among the one-third of Republicans who identify themselves as "born again."

Part D of Table 8.1 addresses a particularly strong relationship between economic anxiety and the presidential vote. All respondents were asked to provide their assessments and expectations regarding their own household's past and future economic experience and prospects, as well as their expectations regarding the economic performance for the nation as a whole. Each question provided a five-point scale.

Respondents were first asked whether the national economy had gotten much better, gotten better, stayed about the same, gotten worse, or gotten much worse. They were also asked whether the previous year's household income had increased a lot, increased somewhat, stayed about the same, decreased somewhat, or decreased a lot. A third question asked whether they expected the next year's household income to get much better, get somewhat better, stay about the same, get somewhat worse, or get much worse. A summary index is constructed as the sum of the responses to each of these three questions, yielding an index that varies from 0 (most pessimistic on each question) to 12 (most optimistic on each question). Thus, an index score of 0 indicates a high level of economic anxiety, and a score of 12 indicates a high level of economic optimism.

We employ the index as a measure of economic anxiety, and the results demonstrate a strong relationship between anxiety and the vote for Trump: 90 percent of the most pessimistic reported voting for Trump, while 82 percent of the most optimistic reported voting for Clinton. The simple correlation between family income and the anxiety index is negative (−0.22). Hence, the anxious were less likely to be affluent. This is not surprising, but it points to an important aspect of Trump's appeal. While those who were economically anxious were more likely to support his candidacy, so were those voters who were more affluent. His candidacy managed to create a coalition that included both affluent and economically anxious citizens, perhaps because many of the affluent did not take his populism seriously.

HOW SHOULD WE ASSESS THE POLITICAL
CONSEQUENCES OF ECONOMIC ANXIETY?

One cannot blame working-class voters for being economically anxious in virtually any of the advanced democratic systems. A common circumstance, shared among all the western democracies, has been an increasing concentration of enormous wealth within an increasingly small group of the population. Regardless of whether one supports Bernie Sanders and his political movement, the objective reality is that wealth has become increasingly concentrated at the expense of an economically vibrant working and middle class. Well-paid working-class jobs are disappearing – an economic and political fact of life across the societies commonly regarded as democratic (Bartels 2008; Piketty and Saez 2003). While the remedy for the problem is open to discussion, the importance of this fact for the lower end of the income scale is incontestable, as well as the implications for the distribution of influence in American politics (Gilens 2014; Gilens and Page 2014).

The analyses of Piketty and Saez (2003) show a steep decline in American income inequality beginning with the Great Depression of the 1930s that was dramatically reversed beginning in the early 1980s. Indeed, inequality levels are currently at or near all-time highs in the modern era of the American economy. These levels of inequality follow a path that is the approximate inverse of the rise and decline of labor union membership. That is, as union membership increased, inequality declined. And as levels of labor union membership declined, levels of inequality increased.

Economic anxiety expresses itself in a variety of ways, and it is readily manipulated by a wide variety of politicians from a broad spectrum of political orientations. In effect, Donald Trump told the economically anxious electorate that the failed Democratic Party and its officeholders were responsible for their anxieties and that he would repair the damage. While Clinton was describing job training programs, Donald Trump was explaining why the problems were a direct result of a "rigged" political system. In this way, Trump, more than Clinton, was able to respond to the anxiety and anger that propelled a major part of the electorate.

Indeed, Trump embraced the anger and anxiety of white populists, incorporating their frustrations as a core element of his campaign appeal. Some might even argue that he stimulated that anxiety as an excuse for voters to support his candidacy when in fact his electoral success is anchored in white racism and racial anxiety. We do not contest the importance of racial hostility and fear, but the expressed economic anxiety is also a response to the reality of rising inequality. Indeed, it is the toxic mix of economic anxiety and racial animus that lie at the heart of Trump's populist appeal. The Trump campaign demonstrated that those who have been left behind economically *do* believe that the system is rigged, and they would rather have a job than a job training program. Moreover, economic anxiety affects not only candidate choice but also levels of support for social welfare programs in general and particularly the ACA.

Indeed, as Part E of Table 8.1 shows, support for repeal of the ACA was closely related to the vote. Ninety percent of those opposing repeal reported voting for Clinton, and 76 percent of those supporting repeal voted for Trump. Quite clearly, support and opposition for the ACA tapped into a fundamental factor driving the dynamics of the campaign. And hence, we turn to a consideration of the factors that lay behind support and opposition for the most important social welfare policy expansion of the past fifty years, and also perhaps the most important factor affecting the outcome of the 2016 election.

Finally, a major part of the election campaign revolved around issues relevant to gender, and the particular features of the election served to amplify the magnitude of a previously existing gender gap in American politics. Hillary Clinton was the first woman to be a major party candidate in the general election, and Donald Trump was the first major party candidate who (unintentionally) recorded his sexually misogynistic beliefs on tape for the nation to hear. Table 8.2 demonstrates the resulting gender gap in voter preferences that persisted at comparable levels across each of the major ethnic groups in American politics.

LOCATING SUPPORT AND OPPOSITION FOR THE AFFORDABLE CARE ACT

The ACA was located at the core of the 2016 presidential election campaign. Tables 8.3 and 8.4 employ data taken from the 2016 CCES to compile a more complete picture of the factors behind support and opposition to the signal accomplishment of the Democratic Party during the Obama administration. Trump's promise to repeal the ACA was a primary element of his campaign, and hence, opinions regarding the ACA are central to the election outcome. Indeed, the common theme that emerges from both tables is the (perhaps surprisingly) lukewarm support that the ACA receives.

TABLE 8.2. *Two-party vote for Trump and Clinton by race and gender*

	Men	Women	Total	N =
All respondents				
Clinton	50.3%	57.1%	53.8%	37,380
Trump	49.6%	42.9%	46.2%	
African American				
Clinton	90.5%	96.5%	93.7%	3,927
Trump	9.4%	3.5%	6.3%	
Asian American				
Clinton	71.8%	76.2%	73.9%	1,170
Trump	28.2%	23.8%	26.1%	
Latino American				
Clinton	73.4%	78.2%	75.7%	2,736
Trump	26.6%	21.8%	24.3%	
White American				
Clinton	40.4%	46.8%	43.6%	29,547
Trump	59.6%	53.2%	56.4%	

Table 8.3 addresses support for the ACA across categories of race and party. The table demonstrates that support for repeal was strongest among whites (57.6%) and weakest among African Americans (34.2%). A narrow majority of the Latino American population supported repeal (51.4%), as also nearly a majority of Asian Americans (45%). Within racial-ethnic categories, support for the repeal varied quite dramatically across party affiliation. Even among Democrats the percentage supporting the repeal of the ACA is perhaps surprisingly high: 25% of white Democrats, 31% of African American Democrats, 38% of Latino American Democrats, and 35% of Asian American Democrats. In short, support for stronger social welfare policy within the context of the ACA falls decidedly short of unanimity even among self-identified Democrats.

THE PERSISTENT PROBLEMATICS OF SOCIAL WELFARE POLICY

The Democratic Party suffered dramatic losses in the 2010 congressional election that came during the middle of President Obama's first administration, soon after the passage of the ACA. It was in the aftermath of those losses that the Senate Democratic leader Charles Schumer addressed the National Press Club and called the successful effort to enact the ACA a "mistake" (Edsall 2015). As a political strategy, passing the Act did not secure the support of a majority of Americans in their hearts or minds or in the voting booth. In short, recapturing the spirit

TABLE 8.3. *Percent supporting the repeal of the Affordable Care Act by party and racial group*

A. Among whites

ACA repeal?	Democrat	Republican	Independent	Other	Not sure	Total
No	75.43%	11.58%	39.63%	31.75%	35.27%	42.44%
Yes	24.57%	88.42%	60.37%	68.25%	64.73%	57.56%
Weighted N =	14,803	13,353	13,822	1,858	2,430	46,266

B. Among African Americans

ACA repeal?	Democrat	Republican	Independent	Other	Not sure	Total
No	69.34%	31.36%	60.81%	67.86%	54.65%	65.68%
Yes	30.66%	68.64%	39.19%	32.14%	45.35%	34.32%
Weighted N =	5,724	287	1,360	112	430	7,913

C. Among Hispanic Americans

ACA repeal?	Democrat	Republican	Independent	Other	Not sure	Total
No	61.71%	18.20%	45.73%	38.30%	42.42%	48.60%
Yes	38.29%	81.80%	54.27%	61.70%	57.58%	51.40%
Weighted N =	2,544	846	1,275	94	488	5,247

D. Among Asian Americans

ACA repeal?	Democrat	Republican	Independent	Other	Not sure	Total
No	64.86%	23.81%	50.72%	50.00%	45.04%	51.36%
Yes	35.14%	76.19%	49.28%	50.00%	54.96%	48.64%
Weighted N =	922	378	696	40	242	2,278

TABLE 8.4. *Percent supporting the repeal of the Affordable Care Act by education and racial group*

A. Among whites

ACA repeal?	No high school	High school	Some college	Two years college	Four years college	Postgraduate	Total
No	40.7%	34.1%	40.3%	38.8%	48.3%	56.4%	42.4%
Yes	59.3%	65.9%	59.7%	61.2%	51.7%	43.6%	57.6%
Weighted N =	1,372	12,650	10,719	4,933	10,246	6,359	46,279

B. Among African Americans

ACA repeal?	No high school	High school	Some college	Two years college	Four years college	Postgraduate	Total
No	49.6%	55.4%	67.2%	63.4%	72.8%	79.4%	65.6%
Yes	50.4%	44.6%	32.8%	36.6%	27.2%	20.6%	34.4%
Weighted N =	254	1,811	2,323	1,116	1,756	659	7,919

C. Among Hispanic Americans

ACA repeal	No high school	High school	Some college	Two years college	Four years college	Postgraduate	Total
No	42.6%	45.1%	48.7%	46.0%	50.0%	61.3%	48.6%
Yes	57.4%	54.9%	51.3%	54.0%	50.0%	38.7%	51.4%
Weighted N =	204	1,162	1,498	628	1,374	382	5,248

D. Among Asian Americans

ACA repeal	No high school	High school	Some college	Two years college	Four years college	Postgraduate	Total
No	51.5%	50.0%	55.0%	42.0%	50.0%	53.6%	51.4%
Yes	48.5%	50.0%	45.0%	58.0%	50.0%	46.4%	48.6%
Weighted N =	33	228	362	150	828	677	2,278

of the New Deal in support of a progressive populist agenda that seeks to enlarge the social welfare state for all citizens has become a decidedly difficult journey. That journey is incomplete, and it has not yet managed to win support for the Democratic Party in the larger electorate, or even to win strong consensual support among rank-and-file Democrats of various ethnic backgrounds.

The CCES survey data show that 8 percent of the population of respondents is uninsured, assuming that the small percentage of respondents who do not know whether they are insured are, in fact, uninsured. (This figure coincides with estimates from the Kaiser Family Foundation, which also suggest that 8 percent of the population was uninsured.) Based on the survey data, 10 percent of the respondents purchase their own insurance. Of those who pay for their own insurance, 39 percent use the ACA exchanges. Hence, approximately 4 percent of the respondent population purchases insurance through the exchanges. The current population of the United States is 326 million, suggesting that approximately 32.6 million purchased their own insurance and 12.7 million people purchased through the exchanges. In addition, a significant proportion of the population was covered by Medicaid expansions through the states. And based on the survey data, 26 million remained uninsured.

The ACA produces enormous benefits for the nation's health-care system as well as for those who are covered, but its coverage is not sufficiently wide and embracing to produce immediate political benefits to its champions. In this context, it is important to recall the Hill-Burton Act of 1946 that provided crucial federal government support for hospital construction.[2] In return, hospitals across the country agreed to provide services to patients who were unable to pay for their medical care. The problem is that these guarantees of health care are expensive for the medical care system, while they do not provide for the quality of ongoing care that is crucial to public health.

In this context, the ACA produces enormous benefits for the health-care delivery system, but its direct benefits are not immediately experienced by large proportions of the electorate. Hence, the provision of public health care has not, as Senator Schumer suggested, produced widespread support among many in the electorate who already enjoy access to high-quality health care.

None of this suggests that the ACA is necessarily a political mistake, but rather that the American electorate has not yet been convinced of the need

---

[2] Senator Lister Hill of Alabama was one of the sponsors of the Act.

for a more expansive health-care delivery system. As Table 8.4 shows, support for the ACA is strongest among the best-educated categories within every racial group. This is, perhaps ironically, a hopeful sign for social welfare advocates over the long term. The highly educated groups are less likely to require health care provided through the ACA, thus suggesting that the groups that need it most support it the least. If the ACA survives, more and more of these who do not currently support it are likely to depend on it in the future, and thus support is likely to increase.

COMPARING EFFECTS ON THE SUPPORT FOR TRUMP AND THE REPEAL OF THE AFFORDABLE CARE ACT

Table 8.5 provides a comparison of the major effects on voting for Trump and supporting the ACA repeal. In both parts of the table, a binary logit model is used, first to address the Trump vote and then to address support for the repeal of the ACA. Each part of the table provides the model coefficients with the corresponding standard errors and *t*-values, as well as the change in the probability of the criterion behavior across the range of the independent variable with other independent variables held constant at mean or typical values. The enormous sample of the CCES virtually guarantees small standard errors and large *t*-values. Hence, the analysis of effect magnitudes becomes particularly important.

Part A of Table 8.5 shows the largest effects on the Trump vote arising due to the respondent's support for the ACA repeal, economic anxiety, and partisanship. Part B of Table 8.5 shows particularly substantial effects on support for the ACA repeal as a function of economic anxiety and partisanship. Hence, and not surprisingly, the vote for Trump and support for the repeal of the ACA appear to travel together.

Economic anxiety, in contrast, is not a partisan behavior except perhaps in its political consequences. Yet in Part B of Table 8.5, we see the strong effect of economic anxiety encouraging individuals to support the repeal of the ACA, while we see that larger family incomes encourage individuals to support the repeal as well. Hence, an economically anxious, lower-income individual is being pulled in opposite directions. The Democratic campaign for the ACA, as well as Clinton's campaign for the presidency, failed to reconcile these conflicting impulses among the population that had the most to gain from the ACA.

TABLE 8.5. *Vote for Trump and support for the Affordable Care Act in the 2016 election*

A. Trump vote in 2016 presidential election by ACA repeal, economic anxiety, income, education, party, born-again identification, and racial-ethnic status. Logit model. N = 34,761.

	Coefficient	*t*-value	Change in probability across range of explanatory variable	(Δ)
ACA repeal	2.32	28.63	0.26–0.78	(0.52)
Economic anxiety	0.43	20.35	0.07–0.93	(0.86)
Family income	0.08	6.28	0.41–0.62	(0.21)
Education	−0.20	7.59	0.64–0.39	(−0.24)
Partisanship	2.36	39.57	0.09–0.91	(0.83)
African American	0.00	3.19		
Latino American	−1.24	7.12	0.49–0.22	(−0.27)
Asian	0.00	2.52		
Born again	0.49	6.17	0.43–0.55	(0.12)
Constant	−3.70	18.93		

B. Support repeal of ACA by economic anxiety, income, education, party, born-again identification, and racial-ethnic status. Logit model. N = 35,717.

	Coefficient	*t*-value	Change in probability across range of explanatory variable	(Δ)
Economic anxiety	0.26	23.97	0.21–0.92	(0.63)
Family income	0.05	7.63	0.55–0.73	(0.13)
Education	−0.13	9.56	0.73–0.57	(−0.15)
Partisanship	1.16	42.36	0.32–0.91	(0.33)
Born again	0.68	14.06	0.67–0.82	(0.16)
African American	0.00	2.34		
Latino American	0.21	2.23	0.62–0.67	(0.05)
Asian	0.00	2.73		
Constant	−1.20	11.75		

WHITE SUPPORT FOR TRUMP IN LOCAL CONTEXTS

American national elections have become increasingly structured by race and ethnicity during the post–World War II era, but the role of race and ethnicity crossed a new threshold during the 2016 presidential election campaign. This was largely due to Trump's efforts to inject racial and ethnic animus into the campaign through a variety of actions: his pledge to build a wall aimed at keeping out illegal migration from Mexico, his criticism of a federal judge based on Mexican ancestry, his refusal to recognize Barack Obama's birth in the United States, and more. Trump's efforts to play the race and ethnicity cards during (and after) the campaign have exacerbated the continuing red state-blue state divide, as well as generating important political fallout across states and local communities. Hence, we conclude our analysis of the 2016 election with a closer look at individual vote choice within the larger context of counties and states.

Table 8.6 employs a logit model to regress the two-party Trump vote among whites on the usual suspects – support for the ACA repeal, economic anxiety, income, education, partisanship, and born-again status. The model also includes the size of two different racial-ethnic concentrations at both the county and state levels: the percent Asian and Latino American and the percent African American.

The results add a new dimension to the previous analysis of Table 8.4. Whites who live in *states* with more substantial racial and ethnic populations are *more* likely to support Trump. Whites who live in *counties*

TABLE 8.6 *Trump support among whites*

	Coefficient	*t*-value	Change in probability across range of explanatory variable[a]	(Δ)
ACA repeal	2.73	48.90		
Economic anxiety	0.46	33.59		
Family income	0.06	6.51		
Education	−0.22	10.92		
Partisanship	2.28	55.88		
Born again	0.73	11.85		
County Asian and Latino American	−1.01	3.38	0.47–0.25	(−0.22)
State Asian and Latino American	0.62	2.00	0.47–0.55	(0.08)
County black	−1.11	3.49	0.47–0.26	(−0.21)
State black	2.02	4.52	0.47–0.69	(0.22)
Constant	−6.43	43.56		

Note: Logit model. N = 24,411.
[a] The range of the county proportion of Latino Americans and Asians is 0–0.96.
The range of the state proportion of Latino Americans and Asians is 0.02–0.54.
The range of the county proportion of African Americans is 0–0.81.
The range of the state proportion of African Americans is 0–0.47.

with more substantial racial and ethnic populations are *less* likely to support Trump. How can these geographically divergent results be explained?

We should not be surprised to see differences in political preferences across ethnic and racial groupings. Trump's proposed policies and his language regarding race and ethnicity were aimed at winning white support. There was very little subtlety in these efforts, but even in the absence of Trump's efforts, there has been substantial variation in voting patterns across racial and ethnic voting groups. The present analysis is not, however, focused on variation *across* groups, but rather *within* one group – white voters in the varying racial and ethnic contexts of counties and states. Hence, the question arises, which whites were most likely to be influenced by these appeals based on race and ethnicity?

The pattern of effects points toward racial and ethnic diversity at the state level increasing the probability of supporting Trump, but racial and ethnic diversity at the county level reducing the probability of supporting Trump. A number of explanations help explain these patterns of effects.

First and most important, political analysts and commentators typically rely on survey data that provide information about individual characteristics, beliefs, opinions, and interests. The enduring problem is that individual citizens do not live their lives in social isolation, and they do not form their opinions in social isolation. Instead, they obtain important information from the social contexts in which they are embedded. If they live in socially heterogeneous or homogeneous neighborhoods or cities or counties or states, they are likely to draw conclusions from the experience that might be either correct or misguided. In addition, individuals communicate their political preferences through a variety of direct and less direct vehicles: conversations at the coffee machine, political yard signs on neighborhood streets, sermons from the pulpit, red caps that say "make America great again," and much more (Huckfeldt 1986, 2017; Huckfeldt and Sprague 1995). Through all these interactions, people gain information and disinformation regarding appropriate political beliefs and opinions.

Second, political and social experience also matters with respect to attitudes regarding racial and ethnic diversity. People who experience racial and ethnic diversity draw conclusions based on that experience, and our results suggest that whites in racially diverse states are more likely to support Donald Trump. It is certainly conceivable that people locate themselves in states based on racial and political criteria. It becomes difficult to explain, however, why people would intentionally locate themselves in a racially or ethnically diverse state because of an ethnically diverse population composition, only to vote for the candidate who demonstrates hostility toward those groups.

Third, the same self-selection argument might be more plausibly made regarding counties – people might locate themselves in counties that are racially or ethnically diverse because they value diversity. And because they value diversity, they may not be the sorts of people who were attracted by the Trump campaign. At the same time, it is equally plausible that people make their residential decisions on other grounds (Brown 1981) and that their attitudes toward racial diversity are positively affected by living in diverse circumstances. Even if they did not explicitly choose to live in a diverse county, living with diversity means that many people become personally comfortable with diverse social surroundings and less inclined to embrace the Trump appeal.

Finally, it is entirely possible to reside in a diverse state but never encounter that diversity directly due to residence in an area that lacks diversity. In such situations, it is more likely that living in a diverse state without experiencing that diversity could lead to racially hostile attitudes – the sorts of attitudes that the Trump campaign implicitly or explicitly endorsed.

This discussion has been motivated in part by the commonplace assumption that people might select their residential locations based on political and racial criteria. While that is a useful counterfactual for this discussion, there is very little evidence to support that assumption. Substantial evidence suggests that politics ranks fairly low on the list of factors that guide the vast majority of individuals in choosing a county or a state. To the contrary, politics is only one among many factors that affect the composition of political discussion networks (Brown 1981; Huckfeldt and Sprague 1995; Huckfeldt, Ikeda, and Pappi 2005). In particular, location in politically diverse environments typically results in politically diverse patterns of social interaction (Huckfeldt 2017).

CONCLUSION

The Democrats lost their hold on the populist vote in 2016, but indeed they have been losing that hold for fifty years. An alternative, far less benign version of populism came to the forefront in the 2016 election – a populism driven by racial hostility that was opposed to an expansion of social welfare benefits, even though the beneficiaries would have included many of the individuals who supported the candidate pledged to repeal the benefit. Hence, in the 2016 election, we have seen populism turned upside down. A populism directed at benefitting economically disadvantaged citizens was replaced by a populism motivated by racial and ethnic hostility that drove a wedge between disadvantaged citizens. In addition to being antidemocratic, that emergent form of populism produces outcomes that do not align with the best interests of many voters who embrace it.

The victorious coalition included solid support among self-identified Republicans with little evidence that the party lost any significant support from nominating a standard-bearer who violated many of the Republican Party's long-term policy commitments. Balanced budgets and the need to defend against an aggressive totalitarian regime that posed threats to political and economic freedom no longer held center stage for the Republican Party's chosen presidential candidate. These concerns were jettisoned along with concerns regarding moral turpitude.

Part of the failure also lies at the feet of the Democratic Party. The party has failed to reassure the economic concerns of an electorate that appears increasingly anxious. Absent a progressive populist agenda that has constructed a coalition among all the socially and economically dispossessed, the economically anxious segment of the white electorate embraced the message of a regressive populist who stimulated and gave voice to racial and ethnic anxieties, thus stoking the fires of racial and ethnic conflict. The solution is to create a multiracial coalition of support for the disadvantaged that confronts the social welfare challenges confronting the nation, but this is the continuing task of reconstruction that has stymied American politics for 150 years (Chernow 2017; Foner 1988; Huckfeldt and Kohfeld 1989).

APPENDIX 8.A

The survey shows that 8 percent of the population of respondents is uninsured, assuming that those who do not know whether they are insured are, in fact, uninsured. That figure coincides with contemporaneous estimates from the Kaiser Family Foundation, which also suggest that 8 percent of the population was uninsured.

Based on the survey data, 10 percent of the respondents purchase their own insurance. Of those who purchase, 39 percent use the ACA exchanges. Hence, approximately 4 percent of the respondent population purchases insurance through the exchanges. The current population of the United States is 326 million, suggesting that approximately 32.6 million purchased their own insurance and 12.7 million people purchased through the exchanges.

In addition, a significant proportion of the population was covered through Medicaid expansions through the states. And, based on the survey data, 26 million remained uninsured.

9

Conclusion: The Dangers of Upside-Down Populism

Sombart's (1906) question continues to resonate politically more than 100 years after it was posed. Our effort has refocused the question away from socialism to ask, "Why is there such a meager welfare state in the United States?" Many explanations for American exceptionalism have focused on individualism, individual initiative, and the frontier spirit. While these offer plausible accounts for the resilience of American capitalism and the resistance to government ownership and interference in capital markets and production, they fall short in explaining the relative absence of social welfare benefits being provided by the American government.

Other western democracies have managed to combine capitalism and private ownership of the means of production with an extensive network of guaranteed social welfare benefits in health, education, and general welfare. Yet, in the American context, the effort to provide universal social welfare benefits has met with mixed success. Most recently, The effort to repeal guaranteed medical insurance coverage for all citizens became a primary issue in Donald Trump's 2016 electoral victory. Indeed, health care was a powerful issue for Trump in his campaign, and even the supporters of Hillary Clinton were far from unanimous in their approval of the Affordable Care Act (ACA). Many explanations for Trump's victory have focused on his populist appeal, but how are we to understand a populist appeal that is aimed at denying social welfare benefits to common citizens?

As we have seen, the history of American politics includes a series of populist movements and politicians, including but not limited to the presidential campaigns of Andrew Jackson, William Jennings Bryan, Franklin Roosevelt, and most recently Donald Trump. Populist movements have also played an important role in state politics, particularly in the southern states. The Folsom organization in Alabama, the Long organization in Louisiana, and the Bilbo organization in Mississippi are compelling examples. Once again, these various populist movements have been wildly heterogeneous. Huey Long has been characterized as an existential threat to democratic politics. Franklin Roosevelt is widely viewed as both a traitor to his class and the savior of American democracy. Bilbo was an outrageous racist. All these politicians constructed populist appeals that were aimed at enlisting the support of working-class and lower-middle-class electorates. In short, these populist appeals to common citizens have been central to democratic politics in the history of the republic, but they come in a dramatic variety of shapes and flavors.

Hillary Clinton attempted to mobilize the Democratic Party coalition based primarily on a traditional version of the Democratic Party's contemporary populist appeal that is centered around business-friendly economic progress coupled with the pursuit of social welfare for American citizens. Bernie Sanders, in contrast, advocated a more aggressive version of that populist appeal aimed at creating an American version of Europe's social democracy, with single-payer medical care and free university tuition. The most dramatic contrast occurred in Donald Trump's populist appeal – a populism that exploited white racial hostility in the construction of a coalition that mobilized widespread support among working-class and lower-middle-class whites.

While Donald Trump may have appeared to be an aberration in American politics, he is certainly not the first American populist to construct a regressive demagogic appeal. He did this by embracing issues that have been at the core of Republican Party platforms and combining them with positions that appeal to socially, economically, and politically disaffected white voters. He reached out to traditional Republican constituencies in a range of important ways, embracing tax reform and tax cuts as well as promising major rollbacks of Obama-era regulatory regimes that were aimed at reversing climate change, stimulating economic competition, and stabilizing financial markets. Perhaps most importantly, he promised to repeal and replace the ACA – the most important social welfare legislation adopted since the establishment of Medicare in 1965.

Some of these positions reflect more or less traditional Republican Party positions regarding small government and free enterprise. In contrast, the pernicious populist appeal came in the form of policy justifications tied to some of the worst Bilbo-like instincts of American politics – the vilification of racial and ethnic minorities. Other positions taken by the Trump campaign diverged from traditionally Republican-supported policies. The absence of trade barriers and low immigration barriers for foreign workers has long been important issues to core supporters of the Republican Party, but Trump advocated restrictions on both immigration and trade. He promised to abandon Obama's commitment to relaxed trade restrictions of the proposed Trans-Pacific Partnership (TPP), as well as to reconsider trade regimes established with Canada and Mexico in the North American Free Trade Agreement (NAFTA). He also promised aggressive restrictions on both legal and illegal immigration, not only from Mexico but from other countries as well. Indeed, Trump turned his back on the internationalist wing of the Republican Party by embracing tough restrictions on trade and immigration while constructing a populist appeal aimed primarily at politically disaffected working-class and lower-middle-class whites.

Trump's appeal found a receptive audience with compelling reasons for their political concerns. The past fifty years have created severe obstacles for the well-being of working-class and lower-middle-class Americans *of all racial and ethnic groups*. Labor unions have nearly disappeared as an influential voice, not only with respect to wages and working conditions but also with respect to relevant domestic issues in American politics. Advances in automation and related production technologies have meant that many well-paying jobs on assembly lines have disappeared. At the same time, a great deal of low-skill employment has migrated offshore to less expensive labor markets. Hence, many Americans are being squeezed by technology, on the one hand, and low wage scales in third-world countries, on the other. And not coincidentally, this has been happening at the same time that unions, unionization, and union membership are in steep decline.

Moreover, income inequality has greatly increased during this period, not only in the United States (Bartels 2008; Hacker and Pierson 2010) but internationally as well (Piketty 2014; Piketty and Saez 2003). Indeed, the difficult circumstances facing many of these working-class and lower-middle-class workers have become increasingly grim, and the problem is not unique to any single racial group or any single country. Trump's strategy was to broaden the base of the Republican Party's traditionally conservative coalition by embracing many of these groups whose political loyalties, fifty years earlier, had been closely linked to the Democratic Party.

The Democratic Party's construction of a working-class coalition during the 1940s and 1950s benefitted from an organizational commitment of the Congress of Industrial Organizations (CIO) and other union organizations to support civil rights (Schickler 2016; Schickler, Pearson, and Feinstein 2010). Trump's appeal to these disaffected voters was different, however, because it was embedded within a clear racial message. Once again, "Making America Great Again" is not an appealing message to groups who are attempting to overcome the racial bias that is embedded in American history. At the same time that Trump's appeal divided the working-class and middle-class Americans by race and ethnicity, Hillary Clinton's appeal to the white working class lacked focus and energy. She never managed to find a message that resonated with these traditionally Democratic voters, or to provide them with a compelling reason to support her campaign. Indeed, some of her primary campaign stumbles came in her effort to reach out to these voters, while her close relationship with Wall Street donors compromised her credentials as a candidate of working-class and lower-middle-class voters. While unions supported the Clinton candidacy, many union members did not.

At this particularly low moment in the history of the Democratic Party, what is the task of the party going forward? As a first step, it must resurrect the good name of populist politics by embracing the problems of working-class and middle-class Americans of all racial and ethnic groups. In short, it must stress the common problems and challenges that create a community of shared interests. The Democrats cannot re-create the labor movement of the 1950s, but it can embrace the cause of the working-class and middle-class Americans. While the Bernie Sanders candidacy failed to secure the Democratic nomination, his candidacy provided a clear diagnosis of the political problems that confront the party going forward.

As we have seen, the Democratic coalition has been transformed from a primarily working-class party to a party that relies most heavily on the support of well-educated professional and managerial occupation classes. The underlying political irony is that well-educated Americans have been among the strongest supporters of the ACA. In short, there is every reason to believe that support for social welfare policy can be combined with an appeal aimed at both middle-class and working-class Americans, as well as the professional-managerial classes. Indeed, the inherent difficulties of even the incomplete repeal of the ACA demonstrate the potential for the resurrection of social welfare policy in American politics. The problem of upside-down populism is not winning the support of upper-middle-class Americans, but rather winning the support of working-class Americans!

This is not to say that upper-middle-class America is motivated primarily by altruism. Rather, the economic downturns in the first decade of the century demonstrated the frailty of America's health-care delivery system. In fact, America does have a primitive public health-care system that provides universal access as a consequence of the Hill-Burton Act passed in 1946. Hill-Burton provides federal funds for building hospitals, but it requires that any hospital built with those funds cannot turn patients away based on their inability to pay. The problem is that Hill-Burton did not provide for the funding of health care beyond the construction costs.

As a consequence, Hill-Burton does not guarantee the successful delivery of health care, but it does put an enormous load on local public health facilities built with Hill-Burton funds. Indeed, during the worst part of the early 2000s recession, when local mental health-care facilities funded by Sacramento County were closed due to a lack of funds, emergency room hallways at the local public hospital were filled with gurneys carrying mental health patients because there was no room anywhere else. A call went out to medical center employees to provide hygiene supplies for patients. This is no way to run public health-care systems, and problems such as these illustrate that public health is in the *public's* best interest, not simply the interests of those who receive the health-care services.

Finally, and perhaps most compellingly for the future of American politics, the Republican Party is in danger of losing its political soul. The party of Lincoln has been compromised by the race-baiting behavior, not only of the current president but also by a series of demagogic Republican politicians. The fortunes of the Republican Party depend on the ability of moderates within the party to recapture control, or at least to maintain their electoral viability. Returning to Okun's argument, the economic well-being of the republic depends on the balance between equality and efficiency, and that balance depends on vigorous, responsible two-party politics.

The Republican Party is crucial to that balance, but its forays into regressive populist politics have undermined its mission. Indeed, massive Republican tax cuts that increase the size of the federal budget deficit are a poor substitute for efficiency. The contemporary Republican Party depends on the support of the solidly Republican South, and that is a crucial part of its current coalition. At the same time, if the party restricts its appeal too narrowly on southern whites, it will lose its appeal to the larger electorate.

George H. W. Bush and George W. Bush, as former presidents of the United States, recognized the disaster that awaits not only the Republican Party but also the nation as a whole, if the Republican Party continues to make an appeal anchored in regressive populism. Once again, to state the point in their own words, "Americans must always reject racial bigotry, anti-Semitism, and hatred in all forms" (*Boston Globe*, August 16, 2017). In short, the trade-off between equality and efficiency lies at the heart of successful democratic politics, and it should serve not only as a candidate's campaign strategy but more broadly as the basis for democratic competition.

In conclusion, our analysis has focused on American political problems, but the larger challenges to democratic politics posed by regressive populism are not uniquely American. Declining birth rates among other economically advanced societies coupled with the increased immigration of individuals fleeing poverty and political violence generate their own implications for relations between and among the new arrivals and members of the existing population. Difficult challenges frequently arise that defy easy remedies, but political responses anchored in regressive populism pose threats for both the future of democratic governance and individual freedom. Just as important, the new arrivals create enormous benefits, replenishing populations that would otherwise be diminished due to declining birth rates, and creating new generations of citizens who make their own contributions for both the economy and the society.

Bibliography

Abramowitz, Alan and Ruy Teixeira. 2009. "The Decline of the White Working Class and the Rise of a Mass Upper-Middle Class," *Political Science Quarterly* 124 (3): 391–422.

Abramson, Paul R., John H. Aldrich, and David M. Rohde. 2002. *Change and Continuity in the 2000 Elections*. Washington, DC: CQ Press.

Abramson, Paul R., John H. Aldrich, and David M. Rohde. 2012. *Change and Continuity in the 2008 and 2010 Elections*. Washington, DC: CQ Press.

Achen, Christopher and Larry Bartels. 2016. *Democracy for Realists: Why Elections Do Not Produce Responsive Government*. Princeton, NJ: Princeton University Press.

Aldrich, John and John Griffin. 2018. *Why Parties Matter: Political Competition and Democracy in the American South*. Chicago, IL: University of Chicago Press.

Alesina, Alberto and Edward Glaeser. 2004. *Fighting Poverty in the U.S. and Europe: A World of Difference*. Oxford: Oxford University Press.

Bartels, Larry M. 2006. "What's the Matter with What's the Matter with Kansas," *Quarterly Journal of Political Science* 1: 201–226.

Bartels, Larry M. 2008. *Unequal Democracy: The Political Economy of the New Gilded Age*. Princeton, NJ: Princeton University Press.

Beard, Charles A. and Mary R. Beard. 1927. *The Rise of American Civilization*. New York: Macmillan.

Benoit, Kenneth and Kenneth A. Shepsle. 1995. "Electoral Systems and Minority Representation," in Paul E. Peterson (ed.), *Classifying by Race*. Princeton, NJ: Princeton University Press, pp. 50–84.

Black, Earl and Merle Black. 2002. *The Rise of Southern Republicans*. Cambridge, MA: Harvard University Press.

Bolling, Richard. 1965. *House Out of Order*. New York: E. P. Dutton.

Bond, Julian. 1990. "In Commemoration of the 25th Anniversary of the Voting Rights Act of 1965; Race and Politics in the Twentieth Century United States: A Participant's Commentary." Paper prepared for delivery before the New England Historical Association, April 21, Pine Manor College, Boston.

Bonica, Adam, Nolan McCarty, Keith T. Poole, and Howard Rosenthal. 2013. "Why Hasn't Democracy Slowed Rising Inequality?" *Journal of Economic Perspectives* 27: 103–124.

Boyd, Thomas M. and Stephen J. Markman. 1983. "The 1982 Amendments to the Voting Rights Act: A Legislative History," *Washington and Lee Law Review* 40(4): 1347–1428.

Brady, David W. and Charles S. Bullock III. 1980. "Is There a Conservative Coalition in the House?" *Journal of Politics* 42: 549–559.

Brand, H. W. 2008. *Traitor to His Class: The Privileged Life and Radical Presidency of Franklin Delano Roosevelt*. New York: Doubleday.

Brooks, Clem and Jeff Manza. 1997a. "Class Politics and Political Change in the United States, 1952–1992," *Social Forces* 76: 389–408.

Brooks, Clem and Jeff Manza. 1997b. "Social Cleavages and Political Alignments: U.S. Presidential Elections, 1960–1992," *American Sociological Review* 62: 937–946.

Brooks, Clem and Jeff Manza. 2007. *Why Welfare States Persist: The Importance of Public Opinion in Democracies*. Chicago, IL: University of Chicago Press.

Brooks, Clem and Jeff Manza. 2013. "A Broken Public? Americans' Responses to the Great Recession," *American Sociological Review* 78: 727–748.

Brown, Thad. 1981. "On Contextual Change and Partisan Attitudes," *British Journal of Political Science* 11: 427–448.

Browning, Rufus P., Dale Rogers Marshall, and David H.Tabb. 1986. *Protest Is Not Enough: The Struggle of Blacks and Hispanics for Equality in Urban Politics*. Berkeley, CA: University of California Press.

Burnham, Walter D. 1970. *Critical Elections and the Mainsprings of American Politics*. New York: W. W. Norton.

Burns, Ken (Director). 1986. *Huey Long*. Washington, DC: Florentine Films.

Cameron, Charles, David Epstein, and Sharon O'Halloran. 1996. "Do Majority-Minority Districts Maximize Substantive Black Representation in Congress?" *American Political Science Review* 90: 794–812.

Carmines, Edward G. and James A. Stimson. 1981. "Issue Evolution, Population Replacement, and Normal Partisan Change," *American Political Science Review* 75: 107–118.

Carmines, Edward G. and James A. Stimson. 1989. *Issue Evolution: Race and the Transformation of American Politics*. Princeton, NJ: Princeton University Press.

Carnes, Nicholas. 2013. *White-Collar Government: The Hidden Role of Class in Economic Policy Making*. Chicago, IL: University of Chicago Press.

Caro, Robert A. 1982. *The Years of Lyndon Johnson: The Path to Power*. New York: Alfred A. Knopf.

Caro, Robert A. 1990. *The Years of Lyndon Johnson: Means of Ascent*. New York: Alfred A. Knopf.

Caro, Robert A. 2002. *The Years of Lyndon Johnson: Master of the Senate*. New York: Alfred A. Knopf.

Caro, Robert A. 2012. *The Years of Lyndon Johnson: The Passage of Power*. New York: Alfred A. Knopf.

Chernow, Ron. 2017. *Grant*. New York: Penguin Press.

Clausen, Aage R. 1973. *How Congressmen Decide: A Policy Focus*. New York: St. Martin's Press.

Cleveland, William S. 1993. *Visualizing Data*. Summit, NJ: Hobart Press.

Crespino, Joseph. 2007. *In Search of Another Country: Mississippi and the Conservative Counterrevolution*. Princeton, NJ: Princeton University Press.

Crespino, Joseph. 2012. *Strom Thurmond's America*. New York: Hill and Wang.

Dahl, Robert. 1961. *Who Governs? Democracy and Power in an American City*. New Haven, CT: Yale University Press.

Dalton, Russell J. 2018. *Political Realignment: Economics, Culture and Electoral Change*. Oxford: Oxford University Press.

Dalton, Russell J. 2019. *Citizen Politics: Public Opinion and Political Parties in Advanced Industrial Democracies*. 7th ed. Washington, DC: CQ Press and Sage Publications.

Desjardins, Lisa. 2018. "Every Moment in Trump's Charged Relationship with Race," *PBS Newshour*. January 12. www.pbs.org.

Donovan, John C. 1967. *The Politics of Poverty*. New York: Pegasus.

Douglas, Paul H. 1971. *In the Fullness of Time: The Memoirs of Paul H. Douglas*. New York: Harcourt Brace Jovanovich.

Edsall, Thomas C. 2015. "Is Obamacare Destroying the Democratic Party?" *New York Times*, December 22.

Edsall, Thomas C. 2017. "The Peculiar Populism of Donald Trump," *New York Times*, February 2.

Elliott, Carl, Sr. and Michael D'Orso. 1992. *The Cost of Courage: The Journey of an American Congressman*. New York: Doubleday.

Evans, Rowland and Robert Novak. 1966. *Lyndon B. Johnson: The Exercise of Power*. New York: New American Library.

Fearon, James D. 2006. "Ethnic Mobilization and Ethnic Violence," in Donald A. Wittman and Barry R. Weingast (eds.), *Oxford Handbook of Political Economy*. Oxford: Oxford University Press, pp. 852–868.

Felzenberg, Alvin S. 2017. *A Man and His Presidents – The Political Odyssey of William Buckley, Jr*. New Haven, CT: Yale University Press.

Flake, Jeff. 2017. "In a Democracy, There Can Be No Bystanders," *New York Times*. November 6.

Foner, Eric. 1988. *Reconstruction: America's Unfinished Revolution, 1863–1877*. New York: Harper and Row.

Foner, Eric. 2005. *Forever Free: The Story of Emancipation and Reconstruction*. Illustrations edited and with commentary by Joshua Brown. New York: Vintage Books of Random House.

Foner, Eric. 2010. *The Fiery Trial: Abraham Lincoln and American Slavery*. New York: W. W. Norton.

Foner, Eric and Joshua Brown. 2005. *Forever Free: The Story of Emancipation and Reconstruction*. New York: Alfred A. Knopf.

Frank, Thomas. 2004. *What's the Matter with Kansas? How Conservatives Won the Heart of America*. New York: Henry Holt.

Frederico Christopher, M. 2004. "When Do Welfare Attitudes Become Racialized? The Paradoxical Effects of Education," *American Journal of Political Science* 48: 374–391.

Gelman, Andrew, David Park, Boris Shor, and Geronimo Cortina. 2010. *Red State, Blue State, Rich State, Poor State: Why Americans Vote the Way They Do*. Princeton, NJ: Princeton University Press.

Gilens, Martin. 1996. "'Race Coding' and White Opposition to Welfare," *American Political Science Review* 90: 593–604.

Gilens, Martin. 2014. *Affluence and Influence: Economic Inequality and Political Power in America*. Princeton, NJ: Princeton University Press.

Gilens, Martin and Benjamin I. Page. 2014. "Testing Theories of American Politics: Elites, Interest Groups, and Average Citizens," *Perspectives on Politics* 12: 564–581.

Gosnell, Harold F. 1935. *Negro Politicians: The Rise of Negro Politics in Chicago*. Chicago, IL: University of Chicago Press.

Gosnell, Harold F. 1937. *Machine Politics: Chicago Model*. Chicago, IL: University of Chicago Press.

Greenhouse, Steven. 2014. "Volkswagen Vote Is Defeat for Labor in South," *New York Times*, February 14.

Groseclose, Tim, Steven D. Levitt, and James M. Snyder, Jr. 1999. "Comparing Interest Group Scores across Time and Chambers: Adjusted ADA Scores for the US Congress," *American Political Science Review* 93: 33–50.

Guinier, Lani. 1992. "The Representation of Minority Interests: The Question of Single-Member Districts," *Cordoza Law Review* 14: 1135–1174.

Guinier, Lani. 1995. "The Representation of Minority Interests," in Paul E. Peterson (ed.), *Classifying by Race*. Princeton, NJ: Princeton University Press, pp. 21–49.

Hacker, Jacob and Paul Pierson. 2010. "Winner Take All Politics: Public Policy, Political Organization, and the Precipitous Rise of Top Incomes in the United States," *Politics and Society* 38(2): 152–204.

Hadley, Charles D. 1985. "Dual Partisan Identification in the South," *Journal of Politics* 47(February): 254–268.

Ho, Daniel E. and Kevin M. Quinn. 2010. "How Not to Lie with Judicial Votes: Misconception, Measurement, and Models," *California Law Review* 98: 813–876.

Hofstadter, Richard. 1955. *The Age of Reform: From Bryan to F.D.R.* New York: Random House.

Holmes, Michael S. 1972. "The New Deal and Georgia's Black Youth," *Journal of Southern History* 38(August): 443–460.

Hood III, M. V., Quentin Kidd, and Irwin L. Morris. 1999. "Of Byrds[s] and Bumpers: Using Democratic Senators to Analyze Political Change in the South, 1960–1995," *American Journal of Political Science* 43: 465–487.

Hout, Michael. 2008. "How Class Works: Objective and Subjective Aspects of Class Since the 1970s," in Annette Lareau and Dalton Conley (eds.), *Social Class: How Does It Work?* New York: Russell Sage, pp. 25–64.

Hout, Michael, Clem Brooks, and Jeff Manza. 1995. "The Democratic Class Struggle in the United States," *American Sociological Review* 60: 805–828.

Huckfeldt, Robert. 1986. *Politics in Context: Assimilation and Conflict in Urban Neighborhoods*. New York: Agathon Press.

Huckfeldt, Robert. 2017. "Interdependence, Communication, and Aggregation: Transforming Voters into Electorates," *PS: Political Science and Politics* (January) 50 (1): 3–11. doi:10.1017/S1049096516002006.

Huckfeldt, Robert and Carol W. Kohfeld. 1989. *Race and the Decline of Class in American Politics*. Urbana, IL: University of Illinois Press.

Huckfeldt, Robert and John Sprague. 1995. *Citizens, Politics, and Social Communication*. New York: Cambridge University Press.

Huckfeldt, Robert, Kenichi Ikeda, and Franz U. Pappi. 2005. "Patterns of Disagreement in Democratic Politics: Comparing Germany, Japan, and the United States," *American Journal of Political Science* 49: 497–514.

Huckfeldt, Robert, Jeffrey Levine, William Morgan, and John Sprague. 1999. "Accessibility and the Political Utility of Partisan and Ideological Orientations," *American Journal of Political Science* 43: 888–911.

Humphrey, Hubert H. 1976. *The Education of a Public Man*. New York: Doubleday.

Inglehart, Ronald. 1977. *The Silent Revolution*. Princeton, NJ: Princeton University Press.

Inglehart, Ronald and Pippa Norris. 2017. "Trump and the Populist Authoritarian Parties: The Silent Revolution in Reverse," *Perspectives on Politics* 15(June): 443–454.

Jardina, Ashley. 2019. *White Identity Politics*. Cambridge: Cambridge University Press.

Jeong, Gyung-Ho, Gary Miller, and Itai Sened. 2009. "Closing the Deal: Negotiating Civil Rights Legislation," *American Political Science Review* 103(4): 588–606.

Judd, Dennis. 1979. *The Politics of American Cities: Private Power and Public Policy*. New York: Little, Brown.

Katznelson, Ira. 2005. *When Affirmative Action Was White: An Untold History of Racial Inequality in Twentieth Century America*. New York: W. W. Norton.

Katznelson, Ira. 2013. *Fear Itself: The New Deal and the Origins of Our Times*. New York: Liveright Publishing Company.

Katznelson, Ira and Quinn Mulroy. 2012. "Was the South Pivotal? Situated Partisanship and Policy Coalitions during the New Deal and Fair Deal," *Journal of Politics* 74(April): 604–620.

Kazin, Michael. 1998. *The Populist Persuasion: An American History*. Ithaca, NY: Cornell University Press.

Key, V. O. 1949. *Southern Politics in State and Nation*. New York: Alfred A. Knopf.

Key, V. O. 1955. "A Theory of Critical Elections," *Journal of Politics* 17: 3–18.

Key, V. O. 1959. "Secular Realignment and the Party System," *Journal of Politics* 21: 198–210.

Kousser, J. Morgan. 1974. *The Shaping Southern Politics: Suffrage Restrictions and the Establishment of the One-Party South, 1880–1910*. New Haven, CT: Yale University Press.

Kousser, J. Morgan. 1999. *Colorblind Injustice: Minority Voting Rights and the Undoing of the Second Reconstruction.* Chapel Hill, NC: University of North Carolina Press.

Kousser, J. Morgan. 2008. "The Strange, Ironic Career of Section 5 of the Voting Rights Act, 1965–2007," *Texas Law Review* 86(March): 667–775.

Leuchtenburg, William E. 2015. *The American President: From Teddy Roosevelt to Bill Clinton.* Oxford: Oxford University Press.

Lewis, Jeffrey B., Keith Poole, Howard Rosenthal, Adam Boche, Aaron Rudkin, and Luke Sonnet. 2020. "Voteview: Congressional Roll-Call Votes Database." https://voteview.com/.

Liebling, A. J. 1978. *The Earl of Louisiana.* Baton Rouge, LA: Louisiana State University Press.

Lodge, Milton and Charles Taber. 2013. *The Rationalizing Voter.* New York: Cambridge University Press.

Loevy, Robert D. 1997. *The Civil Rights Act of 1964: The Passage of the Law That Ended Racial Segregation.* Albany, NY: SUNY Press.

Luce, Edward. 2017. *The Retreat of Western Liberalism.* New York: Atlantic Monthly Press.

Manley, John F. 1973. "The Conservative Coalition in Congress," *American Behavioral Scientist* 17(2): 223–247.

Manza, Jeff, Michael Hout, and Clem Brooks. 1995. "Class Voting in Capitalist Democracies since World War II: Dealignment, Realignment, or Trendless Fluctuation?" *Annual Review of Sociology* 21: 137–162.

Massey, Douglas S. and Nancy A. Denton. 1998. *American Apartheid: Segregation and the Making of the Underclass.* Cambridge, MA: Harvard University Press.

Matthews, Donald R. and James W. Prothro. 1963a. "Political Factors and Negro Voter Registration in the South," *American Political Science Review* 57(1): 355–367.

Matthews, Donald R. and James W. Prothro. 1963b. "Social and Economic Factors and Negro Voter Registration in the South," *American Political Science Review* 57(1): 24–44.

McCarty, Nolan, Keith T. Poole, and Howard Rosenthal. 2006. *Polarized America.* Cambridge, MA: MIT Press.

McPherson, James M. 1982. "Some Thoughts on the Civil War as the Second American Revolution," *Hayes Historical Journal* 3. www.rbhayes.org/research/hayes-historical-journal-some-thoughts-on-the-civil-war.

McPherson, James M. 1988. *Battle Cry of Freedom: The Civil War Era.* New York: Oxford University Press.

McPherson, James M. 1992. *Abraham Lincoln and the Second American Revolution.* New York: Oxford University Press.

Mendelberg, Tali. 2001. *The Race Card: Campaign Strategy, Implicit Messages, and the Norm of Equality.* Princeton, NJ: Princeton University Press.

Mishel, Lawrence and Alyssa Davis. 2014. "CEO Pay Continues to Rise as Typical Workers are Paid Less." Issue Brief #380, June 12. Washington, DC: Economic Policy Institute.

Morris, Edmund. 2011. *Colonel Roosevelt.* New York: Random House.

Mowry, George. 1951. *The California Progressives.* Berkeley and Los Angeles: University of California Press.

New York Times. 2012. "Presidential Election Exit Polls." http://elections.nytimes.com/2012/results/president/exit-polls (accessed February 18, 2020).

Noel, Hans. 2016. "NOMINATE Scores Do Not Measure Ideology, But They Can be Used to Study It: Disentangling Ideology from Party in Roll Call Data." Paper presented at the 2016 American Political Science Association Meetings.

OECD. 2019. *Social Expenditure Update 2019: Public Social Spending Is High in Many OECD Countries.* Paris: OECD Publishing.

Okun, Arthur M. 1975. *Equality and Efficiency: The Big Tradeoff.* Washington, DC: Brookings Institution, pp. vii–xii.

Olson, Mancur. 1965. *The Logic of Collective Action: Public Goods and the Theory of Groups.* Cambridge, MA: Harvard University Press.

Opsahl, T., F. Agneessens, and Skvoretz J. 2010. "Node Centrality in Weighted Networks: Generalizing Degree and Shortest Paths," *Social Networks* 32(3): 245–251.

Piketty, Thomas. 2014. *Capital in the Twenty-First Century.* Cambridge, MA: Harvard University Press.

Piketty, Thomas and Emmanuel Saez. 2003. "Income Inequality in the United States, 1913–1998," *Quarterly Journal of Economics* 118: 1–39.

Piven, Frances F. and Richard A. Cloward. 1971. *Regulating the Poor: The Functions of Public Welfare.* New York: Pantheon Books.

Poole, Keith T. 2005. *Spatial Models of Parliamentary Voting.* Cambridge: Cambridge University Press.

Poole, Keith T. 2007. "Changing Minds? Not in Congress!" *Public Choice* 131: 435–451.

Poole, Keith T. and Howard Rosenthal. 1984. "The Polarization of American Politics," *Journal of Politics* 46: 1061–1079.

Poole, Keith T. and Howard Rosenthal. 1985. "A Spatial Model for Legislative Roll Call Analysis," *American Journal of Political Science* 29: 357–384.

Poole, Keith T. and Howard Rosenthal. 1997. *Congress: A Political-Economic History of Roll Call Voting.* New York: Oxford University Press.

Poole, Keith T. and Howard Rosenthal. 2007. *Ideology and Congress. Second revised edition of Congress: A Political Economic History of Roll Call Voting.* New Brunswick, NJ: Transaction Publishers.

Prignano, Christina. 2017. "Former Presidents George H.W. and George W. Bush Speak Out after Trump Comments," *Boston Globe,* August 16.

Przeworski, Adam and John Sprague. 1986. *Paper Stones: A History of Electoral Socialism.* Chicago, IL: University of Chicago Press.

Purdum, Todd. 2014. *An Idea Whose Time Has Come: Two Presidents, Two Parties, and the Battle for the Civil Rights Act of 1964.* New York: Henry Holt.

Rauh, Jr., Joseph. 1997. "The Role of the Leadership Conference on Civil Rights in the Civil Rights Struggle of 1963-1964," Chapter 2 in Robert D. Loevy (ed.), *The Civil Rights Act of 1964.* Albany, NY: State University of New York Press, pp. 49–76.

Riker, William H. 1982. *Liberalism against Populism: A Confrontation between the Theory of Democracy and the Theory of Social Choice.* Prospect Heights, IL: Waveland Press.

Riker, William H. 1986. *The Art of Political Manipulation.* New Haven, CT: Yale University Press.

Rodriguez, Daniel B. and Barry R. Weingast. 2003. "The Positive Political Theory of Legislative History: New Perspectives on the 1964 Civil Rights Act and Its Interpretation," *University of Pennsylvania Law Review* 151: 1417–1541.

Rothwell, Jonathan. 2017. "Myths of the 1 Percent: What Puts People at the Top," *New York Times*, November 27.

Schickler, Eric. 2001. *Disjointed Pluralism: Institutional Innovation and the Development of the U.S. Congress.* Princeton, NJ: Princeton University Press.

Schickler, Eric. 2016. *Racial Realignment: The Transformation of American Liberalism, 1932–1965.* Princeton, NJ: Princeton University Press.

Schickler, Eric, Kathryn Pearson, and Brian D. Feinstein. 2010. "Congressional Parties and Civil Rights Politics from 1933 to 1972," *Journal of Politics* 72(July): 672–689.

Shafer, Byron E. and Richard Johnston. 2009. *The End of Southern Exceptionalism: Class, Race, and Partisan Change in the Postwar South.* Cambridge, MA: Harvard University Press.

Sombart, Werner. 1976. *Why Is There No Socialism in the United States?* White Plains, NY: International Arts and Sciences Press (Originally published in 1906).

Sonenshein, Raphael J. 1993. *Politics in Black and White.* Princeton, NJ: Princeton University Press.

StataCorp. 2017. *Stata Statistical Software: Release 14.* College Station, TX: StataCorp LP.

Stevenson, Adlai. 1953. *Major Campaign Speeches of Adlai Stevenson.* New York: Random House.

Stiglitz, Joseph E. 2012. *The Price of Inequality: How Today's Divided Society Endangers Our Future.* New York: W. W. Norton.

Stonecash, Jeffrey M. 2000. *Class and Party in American Politics.* Boulder, CO: Westview Press.

Stonecash, Jefrey M., Mark D. Brewer, and Mack D. Mariani. 2003. *Diverging Parties: Social Change, Realignment, and Party Polarization.* Boulder, CO: Westview Press.

Summers, Lawrence H. 2015a. "Comments." Prepared for delivery at 40 Years Later – The Relevance of Okun's Equality and Efficiency: The Big Tradeoff, May 4. Washington DC: Brookings Institution.

Summers, Lawrence H. 2015b. "Foreword," in Arthur Okun, *Equality and Efficiency: The Big Tradeoff.* Washington, DC: Brookings Institution.

Sundquist, James L. 1973. *Dynamics of the Party System.* Washington, DC: Brookings Institution.

Sundquist, James L. 1983. *Dynamics of the Party System: Alignment and Realignment of Political Parties in the United States.* Washington, DC: Brookings Institution.

Teixeira, Ruy and Alan Abramowitz. 2008. "The Decline of the White Working Class and the Rise of a Mass Upper Middle Class." Washington, DC: Brookings Working Paper.

Theriault, Sean M. 2006. "Party Polarization in the US Congress: Member Replacement and Member Adaptation," *Party Politics* 12(4): 483–503.

Tufte, Edward R. 1978. *Political Control of the Economy*. Princeton, NJ: Princeton University Press.

Weakliem, David and Julia Adams. 2011. "What Do We Mean by 'Class Politics'?" *Politics and Society* 39: 475–495.

Whalen, Charles and Barbara Whalen. 1985. *The Longest Debate: A Legislative History of the 1964 Civil Rights Act*. Cabin John, MD and Washington, DC: Seven Locks Press.

Williams, T. Harry. 1970. *Huey Long*. New York: Alfred A. Knopf.

Williamson, Elizabeth. 2016. "A Big Win for Donald Trump in Nevada," *New York Times*, February 24.

Winters, Jeffrey A. and Benjamin I. Page. 2009. "Oligarchy in the United States?" *Perspectives on Politics* 7: 731–751.

Woodward, C. Vann. 1938. *Tom Watson: Agrarian Radical*. New York: Macmillan.

Woodward, C. Vann. 1955. *The Strange Career of Jim Crow*. New York: Oxford University Press.

Wooldridge, Jeffrey M. 2002. *Econometric Analysis of Cross Section and Panel Data*. Cambridge, MA: MIT Press.

Wooldridge, Jeffrey M. 2009. *Introductory Econometrics*. 4th ed. Mason, OH: South-Western Cengage Learning.

Index

9 781108 819459